ALCIBIADES I

Plato

Contents

APPENDIX I. 7
INTRODUCTION. 13
PERSONS OF THE DIALOGUE: Alcibiades, Socrates. 17

ALCIBIADES I

BY
Plato

APPENDIX I.

It seems impossible to separate by any exact line the genuine writings of Plato from the spurious. The only external evidence to them which is of much value is that of Aristotle; for the Alexandrian catalogues of a century later include manifest forgeries. Even the value of the Aristotelian authority is a good deal impaired by the uncertainty concerning the date and authorship of the writings which are ascribed to him. And several of the citations of Aristotle omit the name of Plato, and some of them omit the name of the dialogue from which they are taken. Prior, however, to the enquiry about the writings of a particular author, general considerations which equally affect all evidence to the genuineness of ancient writings are the following: Shorter works are more likely to have been forged, or to have received an erroneous designation, than longer ones; and some kinds of composition, such as epistles or panegyrical orations, are more liable to suspicion than others; those, again, which have a taste of sophistry in them, or the ring of a later age, or the slighter character of a rhetorical exercise, or in which a motive or some affinity to spurious writings can be detected, or which seem to have originated in a name or statement really occurring in some classical author, are also of doubtful credit; while there is no instance of any ancient writing proved to be a forgery, which combines excellence with length. A really great and original writer would have no object in fathering his works on Plato; and to the forger or imitator, the 'literary hack' of Alexandria and Athens, the Gods did not grant originality or genius. Further, in attempting to balance the evidence for and against a Platonic dialogue, we must not forget that the form of the Platonic writing was common to several of his contemporaries. Aeschines, Euclid, Phaedo, Antisthenes, and in the next generation Aristotle, are all said to have composed dialogues; and mistakes of names are very likely to have occurred. Greek literature in the third century before

Christ was almost as voluminous as our own, and without the safeguards of regular publication, or printing, or binding, or even of distinct titles. An unknown writing was naturally attributed to a known writer whose works bore the same character; and the name once appended easily obtained authority. A tendency may also be observed to blend the works and opinions of the master with those of his scholars. To a later Platonist, the difference between Plato and his imitators was not so perceptible as to ourselves. The Memorabilia of Xenophon and the Dialogues of Plato are but a part of a considerable Socratic literature which has passed away. And we must consider how we should regard the question of the genuineness of a particular writing, if this lost literature had been preserved to us.

These considerations lead us to adopt the following criteria of genuineness: (1) That is most certainly Plato's which Aristotle attributes to him by name, which (2) is of considerable length, of (3) great excellence, and also (4) in harmony with the general spirit of the Platonic writings. But the testimony of Aristotle cannot always be distinguished from that of a later age (see above); and has various degrees of importance. Those writings which he cites without mentioning Plato, under their own names, e.g. the Hippias, the Funeral Oration, the Phaedo, etc., have an inferior degree of evidence in their favour. They may have been supposed by him to be the writings of another, although in the case of really great works, e.g. the Phaedo, this is not credible; those again which are quoted but not named, are still more defective in their external credentials. There may be also a possibility that Aristotle was mistaken, or may have confused the master and his scholars in the case of a short writing; but this is inconceivable about a more important work, e.g. the Laws, especially when we remember that he was living at Athens, and a frequenter of the groves of the Academy, during the last twenty years of Plato's life. Nor must we forget that in all his numerous citations from the Platonic writings he never attributes any passage found in the extant dialogues to any one but Plato. And lastly, we may remark that one or two great writings, such as the Parmenides and the Politicus, which are wholly devoid of Aristotelian (1) credentials may be fairly attributed to Plato, on the ground of (2) length, (3) excellence, and (4) accordance with the general spirit of his writings. Indeed the greater part of the evidence for the genuineness of ancient Greek authors may be summed up under two heads only: (1) excellence; and (2) uniformity of tradition--a kind of evidence, which though in many cases sufficient, is of inferior value.

Proceeding upon these principles we appear to arrive at the conclusion that nineteen-twentieths of all the writings which have ever been ascribed to Plato, are undoubtedly genuine. There is another portion of them, including the Epistles, the Epinomis, the dialogues rejected by the ancients themselves, namely, the Axiochus, De justo, De virtute, Demodocus, Sisyphus, Eryxias, which on grounds, both of internal and external evidence, we are able with equal certainty to reject. But there still remains a small portion of which we are unable to affirm either that they are genuine or spurious. They may have been written in youth, or possibly like the works of some painters, may be partly or wholly the compositions of pupils; or they may have been the writings of some contemporary transferred by accident to the more celebrated name of Plato, or of some Platonist in the next generation who aspired to imitate his master. Not that on grounds either of language or philosophy we should lightly reject them. Some difference of style, or inferiority of execution, or inconsistency of thought, can hardly be considered decisive of their spurious character. For who always does justice to himself, or who writes with equal care at all times? Certainly not Plato, who exhibits the greatest differences in dramatic power, in the formation of sentences, and in the use of words, if his earlier writings are compared with his later ones, say the Protagoras or Phaedrus with the Laws. Or who can be expected to think in the same manner during a period of authorship extending over above fifty years, in an age of great intellectual activity, as well as of political and literary transition? Certainly not Plato, whose earlier writings are separated from his later ones by as wide an interval of philosophical speculation as that which separates his later writings from Aristotle.

The dialogues which have been translated in the first Appendix, and which appear to have the next claim to genuineness among the Platonic writings, are the Lesser Hippias, the Menexenus or Funeral Oration, the First Alcibiades. Of these, the Lesser Hippias and the Funeral Oration are cited by Aristotle; the first in the Metaphysics, the latter in the Rhetoric. Neither of them are expressly attributed to Plato, but in his citation of both of them he seems to be referring to passages in the extant dialogues. From the mention of 'Hippias' in the singular by Aristotle, we may perhaps infer that he was unacquainted with a second dialogue bearing the same name. Moreover, the mere existence of a Greater and Lesser Hippias, and of a First and Second Alcibiades, does to a certain extent throw a doubt upon both of them. Though a very clever and ingenious work, the Lesser Hippias does not appear to contain anything beyond the power of an imitator, who was also a careful student of the earlier Platonic writings, to invent. The motive or leading thought of the dialogue may be detected in Xen. Mem., and there is no similar instance of a 'motive' which is taken from Xenophon in an undoubted dialogue of Plato. On the other hand, the upholders of the genuineness of the dialogue will find in the Hippias a true Socratic spirit; they will compare the Ion as being akin both in subject and treatment; they will urge the authority of Aristotle; and they will detect in the treatment of the Sophist, in the satirical reasoning upon Homer, in the reductio ad absurdum of the doctrine that vice is ignorance, traces of a Platonic authorship. In reference to the last point we are doubtful, as in some of the other dialogues, whether the author is asserting or overthrowing the paradox of Socrates, or merely following the argument 'whither the wind blows.' That no conclusion is arrived at is also in accordance with the character of the earlier dialogues. The resemblances or imitations of the Gorgias, Protagoras, and Euthydemus, which have been observed in the Hippias, cannot with certainty be adduced on either side of the argument. On the whole, more may be said in favour of the genuineness of the Hippias than against it.

The Menexenus or Funeral Oration is cited by Aristotle, and is interesting as supplying an example of the manner in which the orators praised 'the Athenians among the Athenians,' falsifying persons and dates, and casting a veil over the gloomier events of Athenian history. It exhibits an acquaintance with the funeral oration of Thucydides, and was, perhaps, intended to rival that great work. If genuine, the proper place of the Menexenus would be at the end of the Phaedrus. The satirical opening and the concluding words bear a great resemblance to the earlier dialogues; the oration itself is professedly a mimetic work, like the speeches in the Phaedrus, and cannot therefore be tested by a comparison of the other writings of Plato. The funeral oration of Pericles is expressly mentioned in the Phaedrus, and this may have suggested the subject, in the same manner that the Cleitophon appears to be suggested by the slight mention of Cleitophon and his attachment to Thrasymachus in the Republic; and the Theages by the mention of Theages in the Apology and Republic; or as the Second Alcibiades seems to be founded upon the text of Xenophon, Mem. A similar taste for parody appears not only in the Phaedrus, but in the Protagoras, in the Symposium, and to a certain extent in the Parmenides.

To these two doubtful writings of Plato I have added the First Alcibiades, which, of all the disputed dialogues of Plato, has the greatest merit, and is somewhat longer than any of them, though not verified by the testimony of Aristotle, and in many respects at variance with the Symposium in the description of the relations of Socrates and Alcibiades. Like the Lesser Hippias and the Menexenus, it is to be compared to the earlier writings of Plato. The motive of the piece may, perhaps, be found in that passage of the Symposium in which Alcibiades describes himself as self-convicted by the words of Socrates. For the disparaging manner in which Schleiermacher has spoken of this dialogue there seems to be no sufficient foundation. At the same time, the lesson imparted is simple, and the irony more transparent than in the undoubted dialogues of Plato. We know, too, that Alcibiades was a favourite thesis, and that at least five or six dialogues bearing this name passed current in antiquity, and are attributed to contemporaries of Socrates and Plato. (1) In the entire absence of real external evidence (for the catalogues of the Alexandrian librarians cannot be regarded as trustworthy); and (2) in the absence of the highest marks either of poetical or philosophical excellence; and (3) considering that we have express testimony to the existence of contemporary writings bearing the name of Alcibiades, we are compelled to suspend our judgment on the genuineness of the extant dialogue.

Neither at this point, nor at any other, do we propose to draw an absolute line of demarcation between genuine and spurious writings of Plato. They fade off imperceptibly from one class to another. There may have been degrees of genuineness in the dialogues themselves, as there are certainly degrees of evidence by which they are supported. The traditions of the oral discourses both of Socrates and Plato may have formed the basis of semi-Platonic writings; some of them may be of the same mixed character which is apparent in Aristotle and Hippocrates, although the form of them is different. But the writings of Plato, unlike the writings of Aristotle, seem never to have been confused with the writings of his disciples: this was probably due to their definite form, and to their inimitable excellence. The three dialogues which we have offered in the Appendix to the criticism of the reader may be partly spurious and partly genuine; they may be altogether spurious;--that is an alternative which must be frankly admitted. Nor can we maintain of some other dialogues, such as the Parmenides, and the Sophist, and Politicus, that no considerable objection can be urged against them, though greatly overbalanced by the weight (chiefly) of internal evidence in their favour. Nor, on the other hand, can we exclude a bare possibility that some dialogues which are usually rejected, such as the Greater Hippias and the Cleitophon, may be genuine. The nature and object of these semi-Platonic writings require more careful study and more comparison of them with one another, and with forged writings in general, than they have yet received, before we can finally decide on their character. We do not consider them all as genuine until they can be proved to be spurious, as is often maintained and still more often implied in this and similar discussions; but should say of some of them, that their genuineness is neither proven nor disproven until further evidence about them can be adduced. And we are as confident that the Epistles are spurious, as that the Republic, the Timaeus, and the Laws are genuine.

On the whole, not a twentieth part of the writings which pass under the name of Plato, if we exclude the works rejected by the ancients themselves and two or three other plausible inventions, can be fairly doubted by those who are willing to allow that a considerable change and growth may have taken place in his philosophy (see above). That twentieth debatable portion scarcely in any degree affects our judgment of Plato, either as a thinker or a writer, and though suggesting some interesting questions to the scholar and critic, is of little importance to the general reader.

ALCIBIADES I
by
Plato
Translated by Benjamin Jowett

INTRODUCTION.

The First Alcibiades is a conversation between Socrates and Alcibiades. Socrates is represented in the character which he attributes to himself in the Apology of a know-nothing who detects the conceit of knowledge in others. The two have met already in the Protagoras and in the Symposium; in the latter dialogue, as in this, the relation between them is that of a lover and his beloved. But the narrative of their loves is told differently in different places; for in the Symposium Alcibiades is depicted as the impassioned but rejected lover; here, as coldly receiving the advances of Socrates, who, for the best of purposes, lies in wait for the aspiring and ambitious youth.

Alcibiades, who is described as a very young man, is about to enter on public life, having an inordinate opinion of himself, and an extravagant ambition. Socrates, 'who knows what is in man,' astonishes him by a revelation of his designs. But has he the knowledge which is necessary for carrying them out? He is going to persuade the Athenians--about what? Not about any particular art, but about politics--when to fight and when to make peace. Now, men should fight and make peace on just grounds, and therefore the question of justice and injustice must enter into peace and war; and he who advises the Athenians must know the difference between them. Does Alcibiades know? If he does, he must either have been taught by some master, or he must have discovered the nature of them himself. If he has had a master, Socrates would like to be informed who he is, that he may go and learn of him also. Alcibiades admits that he has never learned. Then has he enquired for himself? He may have, if he was ever aware of a time when he was ignorant. But he never was ignorant; for when he played with other boys at dice, he charged them with cheating, and this implied a knowledge of just and unjust. According to his own explanation, he had learned of the multitude. Why, he asks, should he not learn of them the nature of justice, as he has learned the Greek language of them? To this Socrates answers, that they can teach Greek, but they cannot teach justice; for they are agreed about the one, but they are not agreed about the other: and therefore Alcibiades, who has admitted that if he knows he must either have learned from a master or have discovered for himself the nature of justice, is convicted out of his own mouth.

Alcibiades rejoins, that the Athenians debate not about what is just, but about what is expedient; and he asserts that the two principles of justice and expediency are opposed. Socrates, by a series of questions, compels him to admit that the just and the expedient coincide. Alcibiades is thus reduced to the humiliating conclusion that he knows nothing of politics, even if, as he says, they are concerned with the expedient.

However, he is no worse than other Athenian statesmen; and he will not need training, for others are as ignorant as he is. He is reminded that he has to contend, not only with his own countrymen, but with their enemies--with the Spartan kings and with the great king of Persia; and he can only attain this higher aim of ambition by the assistance of Socrates. Not that Socrates himself professes to have attained the truth, but the questions which he asks bring others to a knowledge of themselves, and this is the first step in the practice of virtue.

The dialogue continues:--We wish to become as good as possible. But to be good in what? Alcibiades replies--'Good in transacting business.' But what business? 'The business of the most intelligent men at Athens.' The cobbler is intelligent in shoemaking, and is therefore good in that; he is not intelligent, and therefore not good, in weaving. Is he good in the sense which Alcibiades means, who is also bad? 'I mean,' replies Alcibiades, 'the man who is able to command in the city.' But to command what--horses or men? and if men, under what circumstances? 'I mean to say, that he is able to command men living in social and political relations.' And what is their aim? 'The better preservation of the city.' But when is a city better? 'When there is unanimity, such as exists between husband and wife.' Then, when husbands and wives perform their own special duties, there can be no unanimity between them; nor can a city be well ordered when each citizen does his own work only. Alcibiades, having stated first that goodness consists in the unanimity of the citizens, and then in each of them doing his own separate work, is brought to the required point of self-contradiction, leading him to confess his own ignorance.

But he is not too old to learn, and may still arrive at the truth, if he is willing to be cross-examined by Socrates. He must know himself; that is to say, not his body, or the things of the body, but his mind, or truer self. The physician knows the body, and the tradesman knows his own business, but they do not necessarily know themselves. Self-knowledge can be obtained only by looking into the mind and virtue of the soul, which is the diviner part of a man, as we see our own image in another's eye. And if we do not know ourselves, we cannot know what belongs to ourselves or belongs to others, and are unfit to take a part in political affairs. Both for the sake of the individual and of the state, we ought to aim at justice and temperance, not at wealth or power. The evil and unjust should have no power,-- they should be the slaves of better men than themselves. None but the virtuous are deserving of freedom.

And are you, Alcibiades, a freeman? 'I feel that I am not; but I hope, Socrates, that by your aid I may become free, and from this day forward I will never leave you.'

The Alcibiades has several points of resemblance to the undoubted dialogues of Plato. The process of interrogation is of the same kind with that which Socrates practises upon the youthful Cleinias in the Euthydemus; and he characteristically attributes to Alcibiades the answers which he has elicited from him. The definition of good is narrowed by successive questions, and virtue is shown to be identical with knowledge. Here, as elsewhere, Socrates awakens the consciousness not of sin but of ignorance. Self-humiliation is the first step to knowledge, even of the commonest things. No man knows how ignorant he is, and no man can arrive at virtue and wisdom who has not once in his life, at least, been convicted of error.

The process by which the soul is elevated is not unlike that which religious writers describe under the name of 'conversion,' if we substitute the sense of ignorance for the consciousness of sin.

In some respects the dialogue differs from any other Platonic composition. The aim is more directly ethical and hortatory; the process by which the antagonist is undermined is simpler than in other Platonic writings, and the conclusion more decided. There is a good deal of humour in the manner in which the pride of Alcibiades, and of the Greeks generally, is supposed to be taken down by the Spartan and Persian queens; and the dialogue has considerable dialectical merit. But we have a difficulty in supposing that the same writer, who has given so profound and complex a notion of the characters both of Alcibiades and Socrates in the Symposium, should have treated them in so thin and superficial a manner in the Alcibiades, or that he would have ascribed to the ironical Socrates the rather unmeaning boast that Alcibiades could not attain the objects of his ambition without his help; or that he should have imagined that a mighty nature like his could have been reformed by a few not very conclusive words of Socrates. For the arguments by which Alcibiades is reformed are not convincing; the writer of the dialogue, whoever he was, arrives at his idealism by crooked and tortuous paths, in which many pitfalls are concealed. The anachronism of making Alcibiades about twenty years old during the life of his uncle, Pericles, may be noted; and the repetition of the favourite observation, which occurs also in the Laches and Protagoras, that great Athenian statesmen, like Pericles, failed in the education of their sons. There is none of the undoubted dialogues of Plato in which there is so little dramatic verisimilitude.

ALCIBIADES I

PERSONS OF THE DIALOGUE:
Alcibiades, Socrates.

SOCRATES: I dare say that you may be surprised to find, O son of Cleinias, that I, who am your first lover, not having spoken to you for many years, when the rest of the world were wearying you with their attentions, am the last of your lovers who still speaks to you. The cause of my silence has been that I was hindered by a power more than human, of which I will some day explain to you the nature; this impediment has now been removed; I therefore here present myself before you, and I greatly hope that no similar hindrance will again occur. Meanwhile, I have observed that your pride has been too much for the pride of your admirers; they were numerous and high-spirited, but they have all run away, overpowered by your superior force of character; not one of them remains. And I want you to understand the reason why you have been too much for them. You think that you have no need of them or of any other man, for you have great possessions and lack nothing, beginning with the body, and ending with the soul. In the first place, you say to yourself that you are the fairest and tallest of the citizens, and this every one who has eyes may see to be true; in the second place, that you are among the noblest of them, highly connected both on the father's and the mother's side, and sprung from one of the most distinguished families in your own state, which is the greatest in Hellas, and having many friends and kinsmen of the best sort, who can assist you when in need; and there is one potent relative, who is more to you than all the rest, Pericles the son of Xanthippus, whom your father left guardian of you, and of your brother, and who can do as he pleases not only in this city, but in all Hellas, and among many and mighty barbarous nations. Moreover, you are rich; but I must say that you value yourself least of all upon your possessions. And all these things have lifted you up; you have overcome your lovers, and they have acknowledged that you were too much for them. Have you not remarked their absence? And now I know that you wonder why I, unlike the rest of them, have not gone away, and what can be my motive in remaining.

ALCIBIADES: Perhaps, Socrates, you are not aware that I was just going to ask you the very same question--What do you want? And what is your motive in annoying me, and always, wherever I am, making a point of coming? (Compare Symp.) I do really wonder what you mean, and should greatly like to know.

SOCRATES: Then if, as you say, you desire to know, I suppose that you will be willing to hear, and I may consider myself to be speaking to an auditor who will remain, and will not run away?

ALCIBIADES: Certainly, let me hear.

SOCRATES: You had better be careful, for I may very likely be as unwilling to end as I have hitherto been to begin.

ALCIBIADES: Proceed, my good man, and I will listen.

SOCRATES: I will proceed; and, although no lover likes to speak with one who has no feeling of love in him (compare Symp.), I will make an effort, and tell you what I meant: My love, Alcibiades, which I hardly like to confess, would long ago have passed away, as I flatter myself, if I saw you loving your good things, or thinking that you ought to pass life in the enjoyment of them. But I shall reveal other thoughts of yours, which you keep to yourself; whereby you will know that I have always had my eye on you. Suppose that at this moment some God came to you and said: Alcibiades, will you live as you are, or die in an instant if you are forbidden to make any further acquisition?--I verily believe that you would choose death. And I will tell you the hope in which you are at present living: Before many days have elapsed, you think that you will come before the Athenian assembly, and will prove to them that you are more worthy of honour than Pericles, or any other man that ever lived, and having proved this, you will have the greatest power in the state. When you have gained the greatest power among us, you will go on to other Hellenic states, and not only to Hellenes, but to all the barbarians who inhabit the same continent with us. And if the God were then to say to you again: Here in Europe is to be your seat of empire, and you must not cross over into Asia or meddle with Asiatic affairs, I do not believe that you would choose to live upon these terms; but the world, as I may say, must be filled with your power and name--no man less than

Cyrus and Xerxes is of any account with you. Such I know to be your hopes--I am not guessing only--and very likely you, who know that I am speaking the truth, will reply, Well, Socrates, but what have my hopes to do with the explanation which you promised of your unwillingness to leave me? And that is what I am now going to tell you, sweet son of Cleinias and Dinomache. The explanation is, that all these designs of yours cannot be accomplished by you without my help; so great is the power which I believe myself to have over you and your concerns; and this I conceive to be the reason why the God has hitherto forbidden me to converse with you, and I have been long expecting his permission. For, as you hope to prove your own great value to the state, and having proved it, to attain at once to absolute power, so do I indulge a hope that I shall be the supreme power over you, if I am able to prove my own great value to you, and to show you that neither guardian, nor kinsman, nor any one is able to deliver into your hands the power which you desire, but I only, God being my helper. When you were young (compare Symp.) and your hopes were not yet matured, I should have wasted my time, and therefore, as I conceive, the God forbade me to converse with you; but now, having his permission, I will speak, for now you will listen to me.

ALCIBIADES: Your silence, Socrates, was always a surprise to me. I never could understand why you followed me about, and now that you have begun to speak again, I am still more amazed. Whether I think all this or not, is a matter about which you seem to have already made up your mind, and therefore my denial will have no effect upon you. But granting, if I must, that you have perfectly divined my purposes, why is your assistance necessary to the attainment of them? Can you tell me why?

SOCRATES: You want to know whether I can make a long speech, such as you are in the habit of hearing; but that is not my way. I think, however, that I can prove to you the truth of what I am saying, if you will grant me one little favour.

ALCIBIADES: Yes, if the favour which you mean be not a troublesome one.

SOCRATES: Will you be troubled at having questions to answer?

ALCIBIADES: Not at all.

SOCRATES: Then please to answer.

ALCIBIADES: Ask me.

SOCRATES: Have you not the intention which I attribute to you?

ALCIBIADES: I will grant anything you like, in the hope of hearing what more you have to say.

SOCRATES: You do, then, mean, as I was saying, to come forward in a little while in the character of an adviser of the Athenians? And suppose that when you are ascending the bema, I pull you by the sleeve and say, Alcibiades, you are getting up to advise the Athenians--do you know the matter about which they are going to deliberate, better than they?--How would you answer?

ALCIBIADES: I should reply, that I was going to advise them about a matter which I do know better than they.

SOCRATES: Then you are a good adviser about the things which you know?

ALCIBIADES: Certainly.

SOCRATES: And do you know anything but what you have learned of others, or found out yourself?

ALCIBIADES: That is all.

SOCRATES: And would you have ever learned or discovered anything, if you had not been willing either to learn of others or to examine yourself?

ALCIBIADES: I should not.

SOCRATES: And would you have been willing to learn or to examine what you supposed that you knew?

ALCIBIADES: Certainly not.

SOCRATES: Then there was a time when you thought that you did not know what you are now supposed to know?

ALCIBIADES: Certainly.

SOCRATES: I think that I know tolerably well the extent of your acquirements; and you must tell me if I forget any of them: according to my recollection, you learned the arts of writing, of playing on the lyre, and of wrestling; the flute you never would learn; this is the sum of your accomplishments, unless there were some which you acquired in secret; and I think that secrecy was hardly possible, as you could not have come out of your door, either by day or night, without my seeing you.

ALCIBIADES: Yes, that was the whole of my schooling.

SOCRATES: And are you going to get up in the Athenian assembly, and give them advice about writing?

ALCIBIADES: No, indeed.

SOCRATES: Or about the touch of the lyre?

ALCIBIADES: Certainly not.

SOCRATES: And they are not in the habit of deliberating about wrestling, in the assembly?

ALCIBIADES: Hardly.

SOCRATES: Then what are the deliberations in which you propose to advise them? Surely not about building?

ALCIBIADES: No.

SOCRATES: For the builder will advise better than you will about that?

ALCIBIADES: He will.

SOCRATES: Nor about divination?

ALCIBIADES: No.

SOCRATES: About that again the diviner will advise better than you will?

ALCIBIADES: True.

SOCRATES: Whether he be little or great, good or ill-looking, noble or ignoble--makes no difference.

ALCIBIADES: Certainly not.

SOCRATES: A man is a good adviser about anything, not because he has riches, but because he has knowledge?

ALCIBIADES: Assuredly.

SOCRATES: Whether their counsellor is rich or poor, is not a matter which will make any difference to the Athenians when they are deliberating about the health of the citizens; they only require that he should be a physician.

ALCIBIADES: Of course.

SOCRATES: Then what will be the subject of deliberation about which you will be justified in getting up and advising them?

ALCIBIADES: About their own concerns, Socrates.

SOCRATES: You mean about shipbuilding, for example, when the question is what sort of ships they ought to build?

ALCIBIADES: No, I should not advise them about that.

SOCRATES: I suppose, because you do not understand shipbuilding:--is that the reason?

ALCIBIADES: It is.

SOCRATES: Then about what concerns of theirs will you advise them?

ALCIBIADES: About war, Socrates, or about peace, or about any other concerns of the state.

SOCRATES: You mean, when they deliberate with whom they ought to make peace, and with whom they ought to go to war, and in what manner?

ALCIBIADES: Yes.

SOCRATES: And they ought to go to war with those against whom it is better to go to war?

ALCIBIADES: Yes.

SOCRATES: And when it is better?

ALCIBIADES: Certainly.

SOCRATES: And for as long a time as is better?

ALCIBIADES: Yes.

SOCRATES: But suppose the Athenians to deliberate with whom they ought to close in wrestling, and whom they should grasp by the hand, would you, or the master of gymnastics, be a better adviser of them?

ALCIBIADES: Clearly, the master of gymnastics.

SOCRATES: And can you tell me on what grounds the master of gymnastics would decide, with whom they ought or ought not to close, and when and how? To take an instance: Would he not say that they should wrestle with those against whom it is best to wrestle?

ALCIBIADES: Yes.

SOCRATES: And as much as is best?

ALCIBIADES: Certainly.

SOCRATES: And at such times as are best?

ALCIBIADES: Yes.

SOCRATES: Again; you sometimes accompany the lyre with the song and dance?

ALCIBIADES: Yes.

SOCRATES: When it is well to do so?

ALCIBIADES: Yes.

SOCRATES: And as much as is well?

ALCIBIADES: Just so.

SOCRATES: And as you speak of an excellence or art of the best in wrestling, and of an excellence in playing the lyre, I wish you would tell me what this latter is;--the excellence of wrestling I call gymnastic, and I want to know what you call the other.

ALCIBIADES: I do not understand you.

SOCRATES: Then try to do as I do; for the answer which I gave is universally right, and when I say right, I mean according to rule.

ALCIBIADES: Yes.

SOCRATES: And was not the art of which I spoke gymnastic?

ALCIBIADES: Certainly.

SOCRATES: And I called the excellence in wrestling gymnastic?

ALCIBIADES: You did.

SOCRATES: And I was right?

ALCIBIADES: I think that you were.

SOCRATES: Well, now,--for you should learn to argue prettily--let me ask you in return to tell me, first, what is that art of which playing and singing, and stepping properly in the dance, are parts,--what is the name of the whole? I think that by this time you must be able to tell.

ALCIBIADES: Indeed I cannot.

SOCRATES: Then let me put the matter in another way: what do you call the Goddesses who are the patronesses of art?

ALCIBIADES: The Muses do you mean, Socrates?

SOCRATES: Yes, I do; and what is the name of the art which is called after them?

ALCIBIADES: I suppose that you mean music.

SOCRATES: Yes, that is my meaning; and what is the excellence of the art of music, as I told you truly that the excellence of wrestling was gymnastic--what is the excellence of music--to be what?

ALCIBIADES: To be musical, I suppose.

SOCRATES: Very good; and now please to tell me what is the excellence of war and peace; as the more musical was the more excellent, or the more gymnastical was the more excellent, tell me, what name do you give to the more excellent in war and peace?

ALCIBIADES: But I really cannot tell you.

SOCRATES: But if you were offering advice to another and said to him--This food is better than that, at this time and in this quantity, and he said to you--What do you mean, Alcibiades, by the word 'better'? you would have no difficulty in replying that you meant 'more wholesome,' although you do not profess to be a physician: and when the subject is one of which you profess to have knowledge, and about which you are ready to get up and advise as if you knew, are you not ashamed, when you are asked, not to be able to answer the question? Is it not disgraceful?

ALCIBIADES: Very.

SOCRATES: Well, then, consider and try to explain what is the meaning of 'better,' in the matter of making peace and going to war with those against whom you ought to go to war? To what does the word refer?

ALCIBIADES: I am thinking, and I cannot tell.

SOCRATES: But you surely know what are the charges which we bring against one another, when we arrive at the point of making war, and what name we give them?

ALCIBIADES: Yes, certainly; we say that deceit or violence has been employed, or that we have been defrauded.

SOCRATES: And how does this happen? Will you tell me how? For there may be a difference in the manner.

ALCIBIADES: Do you mean by 'how,' Socrates, whether we suffered these things justly or unjustly?

SOCRATES: Exactly.

ALCIBIADES: There can be no greater difference than between just and unjust.

SOCRATES: And would you advise the Athenians to go to war with the just or with the unjust?

ALCIBIADES: That is an awkward question; for certainly, even if a person did intend to go to war with the just, he would not admit that they were just.

SOCRATES: He would not go to war, because it would be unlawful?

ALCIBIADES: Neither lawful nor honourable.

SOCRATES: Then you, too, would address them on principles of justice?

ALCIBIADES: Certainly.

SOCRATES: What, then, is justice but that better, of which I spoke, in going to war or not going to war with those against whom we ought or ought not, and when we ought or ought not to go to war?

ALCIBIADES: Clearly.

SOCRATES: But how is this, friend Alcibiades? Have you forgotten that you do not know this, or have you been to the schoolmaster without my knowledge, and has he taught you to discern the just from the unjust? Who is he? I wish you would tell me, that I may go and learn of him--you shall introduce me.

ALCIBIADES: You are mocking, Socrates.

SOCRATES: No, indeed; I most solemnly declare to you by Zeus, who is the God of our common friendship, and whom I never will forswear, that I am not; tell me, then, who this instructor is, if he exists.

ALCIBIADES: But, perhaps, he does not exist; may I not have acquired the knowledge of just and unjust in some other way?

SOCRATES: Yes; if you have discovered them.

ALCIBIADES: But do you not think that I could discover them?

SOCRATES: I am sure that you might, if you enquired about them.

ALCIBIADES: And do you not think that I would enquire?

SOCRATES: Yes; if you thought that you did not know them.

ALCIBIADES: And was there not a time when I did so think?

SOCRATES: Very good; and can you tell me how long it is since you thought that you did not know the nature of the just and the unjust? What do you say to a year ago? Were you then in a state of conscious ignorance and enquiry? Or did you think that you knew? And please to answer truly, that our discussion may not be in vain.

ALCIBIADES: Well, I thought that I knew.

SOCRATES: And two years ago, and three years ago, and four years ago, you knew all the same?

ALCIBIADES: I did.

SOCRATES: And more than four years ago you were a child--were you not?

ALCIBIADES: Yes.

SOCRATES: And then I am quite sure that you thought you knew.

ALCIBIADES: Why are you so sure?

SOCRATES: Because I often heard you when a child, in your teacher's house, or elsewhere, playing at dice or some other game with the boys, not hesitating at all about the nature of the just and unjust; but very confident--crying and shouting that one of the boys was a rogue and a cheat, and had been cheating. Is it not true?

ALCIBIADES: But what was I to do, Socrates, when anybody cheated me?

SOCRATES: And how can you say, 'What was I to do'? if at the time you did not know whether you were wronged or not?

ALCIBIADES: To be sure I knew; I was quite aware that I was being cheated.

SOCRATES: Then you suppose yourself even when a child to have known the nature of just and unjust?

ALCIBIADES: Certainly; and I did know then.

SOCRATES: And when did you discover them--not, surely, at the time when you thought that you knew them?

ALCIBIADES: Certainly not.

SOCRATES: And when did you think that you were ignorant--if you consider, you will find that there never was such a time?

ALCIBIADES: Really, Socrates, I cannot say.

SOCRATES: Then you did not learn them by discovering them?

ALCIBIADES: Clearly not.

SOCRATES: But just before you said that you did not know them by learning; now, if you have neither discovered nor learned them, how and whence do you come to know them?

ALCIBIADES: I suppose that I was mistaken in saying that I knew them through my own discovery of them; whereas, in truth, I learned them in the same way that other people learn.

SOCRATES: So you said before, and I must again ask, of whom? Do tell me.

ALCIBIADES: Of the many.

SOCRATES: Do you take refuge in them? I cannot say much for your teachers.

ALCIBIADES: Why, are they not able to teach?

SOCRATES: They could not teach you how to play at draughts, which you would acknowledge (would you not) to be a much smaller matter than justice?

ALCIBIADES: Yes.

SOCRATES: And can they teach the better who are unable to teach the worse?

ALCIBIADES: I think that they can; at any rate, they can teach many far better things than to play at draughts.

SOCRATES: What things?

ALCIBIADES: Why, for example, I learned to speak Greek of them, and I cannot say who was my teacher, or to whom I am to attribute my knowledge of Greek, if not to those good-for-nothing teachers, as you call them.

SOCRATES: Why, yes, my friend; and the many are good enough teachers of Greek, and some of their instructions in that line may be justly praised.

ALCIBIADES: Why is that?

SOCRATES: Why, because they have the qualities which good teachers ought to have.

ALCIBIADES: What qualities?

SOCRATES: Why, you know that knowledge is the first qualification of any teacher?

ALCIBIADES: Certainly.

SOCRATES: And if they know, they must agree together and not differ?

ALCIBIADES: Yes.

SOCRATES: And would you say that they knew the things about which they differ?

ALCIBIADES: No.

SOCRATES: Then how can they teach them?

ALCIBIADES: They cannot.

SOCRATES: Well, but do you imagine that the many would differ about the nature of wood and stone? are they not agreed if you ask them what they are? and do they not run to fetch the same thing, when they want a piece of wood or a stone? And so in similar cases, which I suspect to be pretty nearly all that you mean by speaking Greek.

ALCIBIADES: True.

SOCRATES: These, as we were saying, are matters about which they are agreed with one another and with themselves; both individuals and states use the same words about them; they do not use some one word and some another.

ALCIBIADES: They do not.

SOCRATES: Then they may be expected to be good teachers of these things?

ALCIBIADES: Yes.

SOCRATES: And if we want to instruct any one in them, we shall be right in sending him to be taught by our friends the many?

ALCIBIADES: Very true.

SOCRATES: But if we wanted further to know not only which are men and which are horses, but which men or horses have powers of running, would the many still be able to inform us?

ALCIBIADES: Certainly not.

SOCRATES: And you have a sufficient proof that they do not know these things and are not the best teachers of them, inasmuch as they are never agreed about them?

ALCIBIADES: Yes.

SOCRATES: And suppose that we wanted to know not only what men are like, but what healthy or diseased men are like--would the many be able to teach us?

ALCIBIADES: They would not.

SOCRATES: And you would have a proof that they were bad teachers of these matters, if you saw them at variance?

ALCIBIADES: I should.

SOCRATES: Well, but are the many agreed with themselves, or with one another, about the justice or injustice of men and things?

ALCIBIADES: Assuredly not, Socrates.

SOCRATES: There is no subject about which they are more at variance?

ALCIBIADES: None.

SOCRATES: I do not suppose that you ever saw or heard of men quarrelling over the principles of health and disease to such an extent as to go to war and kill one another for the sake of them?

ALCIBIADES: No indeed.

SOCRATES: But of the quarrels about justice and injustice, even if you have never seen them, you have certainly heard from many people, including Homer; for you have heard of the Iliad and Odyssey?

ALCIBIADES: To be sure, Socrates.

SOCRATES: A difference of just and unjust is the argument of those poems?

ALCIBIADES: True.

SOCRATES: Which difference caused all the wars and deaths of Trojans and Achaeans, and the deaths of the suitors of Penelope in their quarrel with Odysseus.

ALCIBIADES: Very true.

SOCRATES: And when the Athenians and Lacedaemonians and Boeotians fell at Tanagra, and afterwards in the battle of Coronea, at which your father Cleinias met his end, the question was one of justice--this was the sole cause of the battles, and of their deaths.

ALCIBIADES: Very true.

SOCRATES: But can they be said to understand that about which they are quarrelling to the death?

ALCIBIADES: Clearly not.

SOCRATES: And yet those whom you thus allow to be ignorant are the teachers to whom you are appealing.

ALCIBIADES: Very true.

SOCRATES: But how are you ever likely to know the nature of justice and injustice, about which you are so perplexed, if you have neither learned them of others nor discovered them yourself?

ALCIBIADES: From what you say, I suppose not.

SOCRATES: See, again, how inaccurately you speak, Alcibiades!

ALCIBIADES: In what respect?

SOCRATES: In saying that I say so.

ALCIBIADES: Why, did you not say that I know nothing of the just and unjust?

SOCRATES: No; I did not.

ALCIBIADES: Did I, then?

SOCRATES: Yes.

ALCIBIADES: How was that?

SOCRATES: Let me explain. Suppose I were to ask you which is the greater number, two or one; you would reply 'two'?

ALCIBIADES: I should.

SOCRATES: And by how much greater?

ALCIBIADES: By one.

SOCRATES: Which of us now says that two is more than one?

ALCIBIADES: I do.

SOCRATES: Did not I ask, and you answer the question?

ALCIBIADES: Yes.

SOCRATES: Then who is speaking? I who put the question, or you who answer me?

ALCIBIADES: I am.

SOCRATES: Or suppose that I ask and you tell me the letters which make up the name Socrates, which of us is the speaker?

ALCIBIADES: I am.

SOCRATES: Now let us put the case generally: whenever there is a question and answer, who is the speaker,--the questioner or the answerer?

ALCIBIADES: I should say, Socrates, that the answerer was the speaker.

SOCRATES: And have I not been the questioner all through?

ALCIBIADES: Yes.

SOCRATES: And you the answerer?

ALCIBIADES: Just so.

SOCRATES: Which of us, then, was the speaker?

ALCIBIADES: The inference is, Socrates, that I was the speaker.

SOCRATES: Did not some one say that Alcibiades, the fair son of Cleinias, not understanding about just and unjust, but thinking that he did understand, was going to the assembly to advise the Athenians about what he did not know? Was not that said?

ALCIBIADES: Very true.

SOCRATES: Then, Alcibiades, the result may be expressed in the language of Euripides. I think that you have heard all this 'from yourself, and not from me'; nor did I say this, which you erroneously attribute to me, but you yourself, and what you said was very true. For indeed, my dear fellow, the design which you meditate of teaching what you do not know, and have not taken any pains to learn, is downright insanity.

ALCIBIADES: But, Socrates, I think that the Athenians and the rest of the Hellenes do not often advise as to the more just or unjust; for they see no difficulty in them, and therefore they leave them, and consider which course of action will be most expedient; for there is a difference between justice and expediency. Many persons have done great wrong and profited by their injustice; others have done rightly and come to no good.

SOCRATES: Well, but granting that the just and the expedient are ever so much opposed, you surely do not imagine that you know what is expedient for mankind, or why a thing is expedient?

ALCIBIADES: Why not, Socrates?--But I am not going to be asked again from whom I learned, or when I made the discovery.

SOCRATES: What a way you have! When you make a mistake which might be refuted by a previous argument, you insist on having a new and different refutation; the old argument is a worn-our garment which you will no longer put on, but some one must produce another which is clean and new. Now I shall disregard this move of yours, and shall ask over again,--Where did you learn and how do you know the nature of the expedient, and who is your teacher? All this I comprehend in a single question, and now you will manifestly be in the old difficulty, and will not be able to show that you know the expedient, either because you learned or because you discovered it yourself. But, as I perceive that you are dainty, and dislike the taste of a stale argument, I will enquire no further into your knowledge of what is expedient or what is not expedient for the Athenian people, and simply request you to say why you do not explain whether justice and expediency are the same or different? And if you like you may examine me as I have examined you, or, if you would rather, you may carry on the discussion by yourself.

ALCIBIADES: But I am not certain, Socrates, whether I shall be able to discuss the matter with you.

SOCRATES: Then imagine, my dear fellow, that I am the demus and the ecclesia; for in the ecclesia, too, you will have to persuade men individually.

ALCIBIADES: Yes.

SOCRATES: And is not the same person able to persuade one individual singly and many individuals of the things which he knows? The grammarian, for example, can persuade one and he can persuade many about letters.

ALCIBIADES: True.

SOCRATES: And about number, will not the same person persuade one and persuade many?

ALCIBIADES: Yes.

SOCRATES: And this will be he who knows number, or the arithmetician?

ALCIBIADES: Quite true.

SOCRATES: And cannot you persuade one man about that of which you can persuade many?

ALCIBIADES: I suppose so.

SOCRATES: And that of which you can persuade either is clearly what you know?

ALCIBIADES: Yes.

SOCRATES: And the only difference between one who argues as we are doing, and the orator who is addressing an assembly, is that the one seeks to persuade a number, and the other an individual, of the same things.

ALCIBIADES: I suppose so.

SOCRATES: Well, then, since the same person who can persuade a multitude can persuade individuals, try conclusions upon me, and prove to me that the just is not always expedient.

ALCIBIADES: You take liberties, Socrates.

SOCRATES: I shall take the liberty of proving to you the opposite of that which you will not prove to me.

ALCIBIADES: Proceed.

SOCRATES: Answer my questions--that is all.

ALCIBIADES: Nay, I should like you to be the speaker.

SOCRATES: What, do you not wish to be persuaded?

ALCIBIADES: Certainly I do.

SOCRATES: And can you be persuaded better than out of your own mouth?

ALCIBIADES: I think not.

SOCRATES: Then you shall answer; and if you do not hear the words, that the just is the expedient, coming from your own lips, never believe another man again.

ALCIBIADES: I won't; but answer I will, for I do not see how I can come to any harm.

SOCRATES: A true prophecy! Let me begin then by enquiring of you whether you allow that the just is sometimes expedient and sometimes not?

ALCIBIADES: Yes.

SOCRATES: And sometimes honourable and sometimes not?

ALCIBIADES: What do you mean?

SOCRATES: I am asking if you ever knew any one who did what was dishonourable and yet just?

ALCIBIADES: Never.

SOCRATES: All just things are honourable?

ALCIBIADES: Yes.

SOCRATES: And are honourable things sometimes good and sometimes not good, or are they always good?

ALCIBIADES: I rather think, Socrates, that some honourable things are evil.

SOCRATES: And are some dishonourable things good?

ALCIBIADES: Yes.

SOCRATES: You mean in such a case as the following:--In time of war, men have been wounded or have died in rescuing a companion or kinsman, when others who have neglected the duty of rescuing them have escaped in safety?

ALCIBIADES: True.

SOCRATES: And to rescue another under such circumstances is honourable, in respect of the attempt to save those whom we ought to save; and this is courage?

ALCIBIADES: True.

SOCRATES: But evil in respect of death and wounds?

ALCIBIADES: Yes.

SOCRATES: And the courage which is shown in the rescue is one thing, and the death another?

ALCIBIADES: Certainly.

SOCRATES: Then the rescue of one's friends is honourable in one point of view, but evil in another?

ALCIBIADES: True.

SOCRATES: And if honourable, then also good: Will you consider now whether I may not be right, for you were acknowledging that the courage which is shown in the rescue is honourable? Now is this courage good or evil? Look at the matter thus: which would you rather choose, good or evil?

ALCIBIADES: Good.

SOCRATES: And the greatest goods you would be most ready to choose, and would least like to be deprived of them?

ALCIBIADES: Certainly.

SOCRATES: What would you say of courage? At what price would you be willing to be deprived of courage?

ALCIBIADES: I would rather die than be a coward.

SOCRATES: Then you think that cowardice is the worst of evils?

ALCIBIADES: I do.

SOCRATES: As bad as death, I suppose?

ALCIBIADES: Yes.

SOCRATES: And life and courage are the extreme opposites of death and cowardice?

ALCIBIADES: Yes.

SOCRATES: And they are what you would most desire to have, and their opposites you would least desire?

ALCIBIADES: Yes.

SOCRATES: Is this because you think life and courage the best, and death and cowardice the worst?

ALCIBIADES: Yes.

SOCRATES: And you would term the rescue of a friend in battle honourable, in as much as courage does a good work?

ALCIBIADES: I should.

SOCRATES: But evil because of the death which ensues?

ALCIBIADES: Yes.

SOCRATES: Might we not describe their different effects as follows:--You may call either of them evil in respect of the evil which is the result, and good in respect of the good which is the result of either of them?

ALCIBIADES: Yes.

SOCRATES: And they are honourable in so far as they are good, and dishonourable in so far as they are evil?

ALCIBIADES: True.

SOCRATES: Then when you say that the rescue of a friend in battle is honourable and yet evil, that is equivalent to saying that the rescue is good and yet evil?

ALCIBIADES: I believe that you are right, Socrates.

SOCRATES: Nothing honourable, regarded as honourable, is evil; nor anything base, regarded as base, good.

ALCIBIADES: Clearly not.

SOCRATES: Look at the matter yet once more in a further light: he who acts honourably acts well?

ALCIBIADES: Yes.

SOCRATES: And he who acts well is happy?

ALCIBIADES: Of course.

SOCRATES: And the happy are those who obtain good?

ALCIBIADES: True.

SOCRATES: And they obtain good by acting well and honourably?

ALCIBIADES: Yes.

SOCRATES: Then acting well is a good?

ALCIBIADES: Certainly.

SOCRATES: And happiness is a good?

ALCIBIADES: Yes.

SOCRATES: Then the good and the honourable are again identified.

ALCIBIADES: Manifestly.

SOCRATES: Then, if the argument holds, what we find to be honourable we shall also find to be good?

ALCIBIADES: Certainly.

SOCRATES: And is the good expedient or not?

ALCIBIADES: Expedient.

SOCRATES: Do you remember our admissions about the just?

ALCIBIADES: Yes; if I am not mistaken, we said that those who acted justly must also act honourably.

SOCRATES: And the honourable is the good?

ALCIBIADES: Yes.

SOCRATES: And the good is expedient?

ALCIBIADES: Yes.

SOCRATES: Then, Alcibiades, the just is expedient?

ALCIBIADES: I should infer so.

SOCRATES: And all this I prove out of your own mouth, for I ask and you answer?

ALCIBIADES: I must acknowledge it to be true.

SOCRATES: And having acknowledged that the just is the same as the expedient, are you not (let me ask) prepared to ridicule any one who, pretending to understand the principles of justice and injustice, gets up to advise the noble Athenians or the ignoble Peparethians, that the just may be the evil?

ALCIBIADES: I solemnly declare, Socrates, that I do not know what I am saying. Verily, I am in a strange state, for when you put questions to me I am of different minds in successive instants.

SOCRATES: And are you not aware of the nature of this perplexity, my friend?

ALCIBIADES: Indeed I am not.

SOCRATES: Do you suppose that if some one were to ask you whether you have two eyes or three, or two hands or four, or anything of that sort, you would then be of different minds in successive instants?

ALCIBIADES: I begin to distrust myself, but still I do not suppose that I should.

SOCRATES: You would feel no doubt; and for this reason--because you would know?

ALCIBIADES: I suppose so.

SOCRATES: And the reason why you involuntarily contradict yourself is clearly that you are ignorant?

ALCIBIADES: Very likely.

SOCRATES: And if you are perplexed in answering about just and unjust, honourable and dishonourable, good and evil, expedient and inexpedient, the reason is that you are ignorant of them, and therefore in perplexity. Is not that clear?

ALCIBIADES: I agree.

SOCRATES: But is this always the case, and is a man necessarily perplexed about that of which he has no knowledge?

ALCIBIADES: Certainly he is.

SOCRATES: And do you know how to ascend into heaven?

ALCIBIADES: Certainly not.

SOCRATES: And in this case, too, is your judgment perplexed?

ALCIBIADES: No.

SOCRATES: Do you see the reason why, or shall I tell you?

ALCIBIADES: Tell me.

SOCRATES: The reason is, that you not only do not know, my friend, but you do not think that you know.

ALCIBIADES: There again; what do you mean?

SOCRATES: Ask yourself; are you in any perplexity about things of which you are ignorant? You know, for example, that you know nothing about the preparation of food.

ALCIBIADES: Very true.

SOCRATES: And do you think and perplex yourself about the preparation of food: or do you leave that to some one who understands the art?

ALCIBIADES: The latter.

SOCRATES: Or if you were on a voyage, would you bewilder yourself by considering whether the rudder is to be drawn inwards or outwards, or do you leave that to the pilot, and do nothing?

ALCIBIADES: It would be the concern of the pilot.

SOCRATES: Then you are not perplexed about what you do not know, if you know that you do not know it?

ALCIBIADES: I imagine not.

SOCRATES: Do you not see, then, that mistakes in life and practice are likewise to be attributed to the ignorance which has conceit of knowledge?

ALCIBIADES: Once more, what do you mean?

SOCRATES: I suppose that we begin to act when we think that we know what we are doing?

ALCIBIADES: Yes.

SOCRATES: But when people think that they do not know, they entrust their business to others?

ALCIBIADES: Yes.

SOCRATES: And so there is a class of ignorant persons who do not make mistakes in life, because they trust others about things of which they are ignorant?

ALCIBIADES: True.

SOCRATES: Who, then, are the persons who make mistakes? They cannot, of course, be those who know?

ALCIBIADES: Certainly not.

SOCRATES: But if neither those who know, nor those who know that they do not know, make mistakes, there remain those only who do not know and think that they know.

ALCIBIADES: Yes, only those.

SOCRATES: Then this is ignorance of the disgraceful sort which is mischievous?

ALCIBIADES: Yes.

SOCRATES: And most mischievous and most disgraceful when having to do with the greatest matters?

ALCIBIADES: By far.

SOCRATES: And can there be any matters greater than the just, the honourable, the good, and the expedient?

ALCIBIADES: There cannot be.

SOCRATES: And these, as you were saying, are what perplex you?

ALCIBIADES: Yes.

SOCRATES: But if you are perplexed, then, as the previous argument has shown, you are not only ignorant of the greatest matters, but being ignorant you fancy that you know them?

ALCIBIADES: I fear that you are right.

SOCRATES: And now see what has happened to you, Alcibiades! I hardly like to speak of your evil case, but as we are alone I will: My good friend, you are wedded to ignorance of the most disgraceful kind, and of this you are convicted, not by me, but out of your own mouth and by your own argument; wherefore also you rush into politics before you are educated. Neither is your case to be deemed singular. For I might say the same of almost all our statesmen, with the exception, perhaps of your guardian, Pericles.

ALCIBIADES: Yes, Socrates; and Pericles is said not to have got his wisdom by the light of nature, but to have associated with several of the philosophers; with Pythocleides, for example, and with Anaxagoras, and now in advanced life with Damon, in the hope of gaining wisdom.

SOCRATES: Very good; but did you ever know a man wise in anything who was unable to impart his particular wisdom? For example, he who taught you letters was not only wise, but he made you and any others whom he liked wise.

ALCIBIADES: Yes.

SOCRATES: And you, whom he taught, can do the same?

ALCIBIADES: True.

SOCRATES: And in like manner the harper and gymnastic-master?

ALCIBIADES: Certainly.

SOCRATES: When a person is enabled to impart knowledge to another, he thereby gives an excellent proof of his own understanding of any matter.

ALCIBIADES: I agree.

SOCRATES: Well, and did Pericles make any one wise; did he begin by making his sons wise?

ALCIBIADES: But, Socrates, if the two sons of Pericles were simpletons, what has that to do with the matter?

SOCRATES: Well, but did he make your brother, Cleinias, wise?

ALCIBIADES: Cleinias is a madman; there is no use in talking of him.

SOCRATES: But if Cleinias is a madman and the two sons of Pericles were simpletons, what reason can be given why he neglects you, and lets you be as you are?

ALCIBIADES: I believe that I am to blame for not listening to him.

SOCRATES: But did you ever hear of any other Athenian or foreigner, bond or free, who was deemed to have grown wiser in the society of Pericles,--as I might cite Pythodorus, the son of Isolochus, and Callias, the son of Calliades, who have grown wiser in the society of Zeno, for which privilege they have each of them paid him the sum of a hundred minae (about 406 pounds sterling) to the increase of their wisdom and fame.

ALCIBIADES: I certainly never did hear of any one.

SOCRATES: Well, and in reference to your own case, do you mean to remain as you are, or will you take some pains about yourself?

ALCIBIADES: With your aid, Socrates, I will. And indeed, when I hear you speak, the truth of what you are saying strikes home to me, and I agree with you, for our statesmen, all but a few, do appear to be quite uneducated.

SOCRATES: What is the inference?

ALCIBIADES: Why, that if they were educated they would be trained athletes, and he who means to rival them ought to have knowledge and experience when he attacks them; but now, as they have become politicians without any special training, why should I have the trouble of learning and practising? For I know well that by the light of nature I shall get the better of them.

SOCRATES: My dear friend, what a sentiment! And how unworthy of your noble form and your high estate!

ALCIBIADES: What do you mean, Socrates; why do you say so?

SOCRATES: I am grieved when I think of our mutual love.

ALCIBIADES: At what?

SOCRATES: At your fancying that the contest on which you are entering is with people here.

ALCIBIADES: Why, what others are there?

SOCRATES: Is that a question which a magnanimous soul should ask?

ALCIBIADES: Do you mean to say that the contest is not with these?

SOCRATES: And suppose that you were going to steer a ship into action, would you only aim at being the best pilot on board? Would you not, while acknowledging that you must possess this degree of excellence, rather look to your antagonists, and not, as you are now doing, to your fellow combatants? You ought to be so far above these latter, that they will not even dare to be your rivals; and, being regarded by you as inferiors, will do battle for you against the enemy; this is the kind of superiority which you must establish over them, if you mean to accomplish any noble action really worthy of yourself and of the state.

ALCIBIADES: That would certainly be my aim.

SOCRATES: Verily, then, you have good reason to be satisfied, if you are better than the soldiers; and you need not, when you are their superior and have your thoughts and actions fixed upon them, look away to the generals of the enemy.

ALCIBIADES: Of whom are you speaking, Socrates?

SOCRATES: Why, you surely know that our city goes to war now and then with the Lacedaemonians and with the great king?

ALCIBIADES: True enough.

SOCRATES: And if you meant to be the ruler of this city, would you not be right in considering that the Lacedaemonian and Persian king were your true rivals?

ALCIBIADES: I believe that you are right.

SOCRATES: Oh no, my friend, I am quite wrong, and I think that you ought rather to turn your attention to Midias the quail-breeder and others like him, who manage our politics; in whom, as the women would remark, you may still see the slaves' cut of hair, cropping out in their minds as well as on their pates; and they come with their barbarous lingo to flatter us and not to rule us. To these, I say, you should look, and then you need not trouble yourself about your own fitness to contend in such a noble arena: there is no reason why you should either learn what has to be learned, or practise what has to be practised, and only when thoroughly prepared enter on a political career.

ALCIBIADES: There, I think, Socrates, that you are right; I do not suppose, however, that the Spartan generals or the great king are really different from anybody else.

SOCRATES: But, my dear friend, do consider what you are saying.

ALCIBIADES: What am I to consider?

SOCRATES: In the first place, will you be more likely to take care of yourself, if you are in a wholesome fear and dread of them, or if you are not?

ALCIBIADES: Clearly, if I have such a fear of them.

SOCRATES: And do you think that you will sustain any injury if you take care of yourself?

ALCIBIADES: No, I shall be greatly benefited.

SOCRATES: And this is one very important respect in which that notion of yours is bad.

ALCIBIADES: True.

SOCRATES: In the next place, consider that what you say is probably false.

ALCIBIADES: How so?

SOCRATES: Let me ask you whether better natures are likely to be found in noble races or not in noble races?

ALCIBIADES: Clearly in noble races.

SOCRATES: Are not those who are well born and well bred most likely to be perfect in virtue?

ALCIBIADES: Certainly.

SOCRATES: Then let us compare our antecedents with those of the Lacedaemonian and Persian kings; are they inferior to us in descent? Have we not heard that the former are sprung from Heracles, and the latter from Achaemenes, and that the race of Heracles and the race of Achaemenes go back to Perseus, son of Zeus?

ALCIBIADES: Why, so does mine go back to Eurysaces, and he to Zeus!

SOCRATES: And mine, noble Alcibiades, to Daedalus, and he to Hephaestus, son of Zeus. But, for all that, we are far inferior to them. For they are descended 'from Zeus,' through a line of kings--either kings of Argos and Lacedaemon, or kings of Persia, a country which the descendants of Achaemenes have always possessed, besides being at various times sovereigns of Asia, as they now are; whereas, we and our fathers were but private persons. How ridiculous would you be thought if you were to make a display of your ancestors and of Salamis the island of Eurysaces, or of Aegina, the habitation of the still more ancient Aeacus, before Artaxerxes, son of Xerxes. You should consider how inferior we are to them both in the derivation of our birth and in other particulars. Did you never observe how great is the property of the Spartan kings? And their wives are under the guardianship of the Ephori, who are public officers and watch over them, in order to preserve as far as possible the purity of the Heracleid blood. Still greater is the difference among the Persians; for no one entertains a suspicion that the father of a prince of Persia can be any one but the king. Such is the awe which invests the person of the queen, that any other guard is needless. And when the heir of the kingdom is born, all the subjects of the king feast; and the day of his birth is for ever afterwards kept as a holiday and time of sacrifice by all Asia; whereas, when you and I were born, Alcibiades, as the comic poet says, the neighbours hardly knew of the important event. After the birth of the royal child, he is tended, not by a good-for-nothing woman-nurse, but by the best of the royal eunuchs, who are charged with the care of him, and especially with the fashioning and right formation of his limbs, in order that he may be as shapely as possible; which being their calling, they are held in great honour. And when the young prince is seven years old he is put upon a horse and taken to the riding-masters, and begins to go out hunting. And at fourteen years of age he is handed over to the royal schoolmasters, as they are termed: these are four chosen men, reputed to be the best among the Persians of a certain age; and one of them is the wisest, another the justest, a third the most temperate, and a fourth the most valiant. The first instructs him in the magianism of Zoroaster, the son of Oromasus, which is the worship of the Gods, and teaches him also the duties of his royal office; the second, who is the justest, teaches him always to speak the truth; the third, or most temperate, forbids him to allow any pleasure to be lord over him, that he may be accustomed to be a freeman and king indeed,--lord of himself first, and not a slave; the most valiant trains him to be bold and fearless, telling him that if he fears he is to deem himself a slave; whereas Pericles gave you, Alcibiades, for a tutor Zopyrus the Thracian, a slave of his who was past all other work. I might enlarge on the nurture and education of your rivals, but that would be tedious; and what I have said is a sufficient sample of what remains to be said. I have only to remark, by way of contrast, that no one cares about your birth or nurture or education, or, I may say, about that of any other Athenian, unless he has a lover who looks after him. And if you cast an eye on the wealth, the luxury, the garments with their flowing trains, the anointings with myrrh, the multitudes of attendants, and all the other bravery of the Persians, you will be ashamed when you discern your own inferiority; or if you look at the temperance and orderliness and ease and grace and magnanimity and courage and endurance and love of toil and desire of glory and ambition of the Lacedaemonians--in all these respects you will see that you are but a child in comparison of them. Even in the matter of wealth, if you value yourself upon that, I must reveal to you how you stand; for if you form an estimate of the wealth of the Lacedaemonians, you will see that our possessions fall far short of theirs. For no one here can compete with them either in the extent and fertility of their own and the Messenian territory, or in the number of their slaves, and especially of the Helots, or of their horses, or of the animals which feed on the Messenian pastures. But I have said enough of this: and as to gold and silver, there is more of them in Lacedaemon than in all the rest of Hellas, for during many generations gold has been always flowing in to them from the whole Hellenic world, and often from the barbarian also, and never going out, as in the fable of Aesop the fox said to the lion, 'The prints of the feet of those going in are distinct enough;' but who ever saw the trace of money going out of Lacedaemon? And therefore you may safely infer that the inhabitants are the richest of the Hellenes in gold and silver, and that their kings are the richest of them, for they have a larger share of these things, and they have also a tribute paid to them which is very considerable. Yet the Spartan wealth, though great in comparison of the wealth of the other Hellenes, is as nothing in comparison of that of the Persians and their kings. Why, I have been informed by a credible person who went up to the king (at Susa), that he passed through a large tract of excellent land, extending for nearly a day's journey, which the people of the country called the queen's girdle, and another, which they called her veil; and several other fair and fertile districts, which were reserved for the adornment of the queen, and are named after her several habiliments. Now, I cannot help thinking to myself, What if some one were to go to Amestris, the wife of Xerxes and mother of Artaxerxes, and say to her, There is a certain Dinomache, whose whole wardrobe is not worth fifty minae--and that will be more than the value--and she has a son who is possessed of a three-hundred acre patch at Erchiae, and he has a mind to go to war with your son--would she not wonder to what this Alcibiades trusts for success in the conflict? 'He must rely,' she would say to herself, 'upon his training and wisdom--these are the things which Hellenes value.' And if she heard that this Alcibiades who is making the attempt is not as yet twenty years old, and is wholly uneducated, and when his lover tells him that he ought to get education and training first, and then go and fight the king, he refuses, and says that he is well enough as he is, would she not be amazed, and ask 'On what, then, does the youth rely?' And if we replied: He relies on his beauty, and stature, and birth, and mental endowments, she would think that we were mad, Alcibiades, when she compared the advantages which you possess with those of her own people. And I believe that even Lampido, the daughter of Leotychides, the wife of Archidamus and mother of Agis, all of whom were kings, would have the same feeling; if, in your present uneducated state, you were to turn your thoughts against her son, she too would be equally astonished. But how disgraceful, that we should not have as high a notion of what is required in us as our enemies' wives and mothers have of the qualities which are required in their assailants! O my friend, be persuaded by me, and hear the Delphian inscription, 'Know thyself'--not the men whom you think, but these kings are our rivals, and we can only overcome them by pains and skill. And if you fail in the required qualities, you will fail also in becoming renowned among Hellenes and Barbarians, which you seem to desire more than any other man ever desired anything.

ALCIBIADES: I entirely believe you; but what are the sort of pains which are required, Socrates,--can you tell me?

SOCRATES: Yes, I can; but we must take counsel together concerning the manner in which both of us may be most improved. For what I am telling you of the necessity of education applies to myself as well as to you; and there is only one point in which I have an advantage over you.

ALCIBIADES: What is that?

SOCRATES: I have a guardian who is better and wiser than your guardian, Pericles.

ALCIBIADES: Who is he, Socrates?

SOCRATES: God, Alcibiades, who up to this day has not allowed me to converse with you; and he inspires in me the faith that I am especially designed to bring you to honour.

ALCIBIADES: You are jesting, Socrates.

SOCRATES: Perhaps, at any rate, I am right in saying that all men greatly need pains and care, and you and I above all men.

ALCIBIADES: You are not far wrong about me.

SOCRATES: And certainly not about myself.

ALCIBIADES: But what can we do?

SOCRATES: There must be no hesitation or cowardice, my friend.

ALCIBIADES: That would not become us, Socrates.

SOCRATES: No, indeed, and we ought to take counsel together: for do we not wish to be as good as possible?

ALCIBIADES: We do.

SOCRATES: In what sort of virtue?

ALCIBIADES: Plainly, in the virtue of good men.

SOCRATES: Who are good in what?

ALCIBIADES: Those, clearly, who are good in the management of affairs.

SOCRATES: What sort of affairs? Equestrian affairs?

ALCIBIADES: Certainly not.

SOCRATES: You mean that about them we should have recourse to horsemen?

ALCIBIADES: Yes.

SOCRATES: Well, naval affairs?

ALCIBIADES: No.

SOCRATES: You mean that we should have recourse to sailors about them?

ALCIBIADES: Yes.

SOCRATES: Then what affairs? And who do them?

ALCIBIADES: The affairs which occupy Athenian gentlemen.

SOCRATES: And when you speak of gentlemen, do you mean the wise or the unwise?

ALCIBIADES: The wise.

SOCRATES: And a man is good in respect of that in which he is wise?

ALCIBIADES: Yes.

SOCRATES: And evil in respect of that in which he is unwise?

ALCIBIADES: Certainly.

SOCRATES: The shoemaker, for example, is wise in respect of the making of shoes?

ALCIBIADES: Yes.

SOCRATES: Then he is good in that?

ALCIBIADES: He is.

SOCRATES: But in respect of the making of garments he is unwise?

ALCIBIADES: Yes.

SOCRATES: Then in that he is bad?

ALCIBIADES: Yes.

SOCRATES: Then upon this view of the matter the same man is good and also bad?

ALCIBIADES: True.

SOCRATES: But would you say that the good are the same as the bad?

ALCIBIADES: Certainly not.

SOCRATES: Then whom do you call the good?

ALCIBIADES: I mean by the good those who are able to rule in the city.

SOCRATES: Not, surely, over horses?

ALCIBIADES: Certainly not.
SOCRATES: But over men?
ALCIBIADES: Yes.
SOCRATES: When they are sick?
ALCIBIADES: No.
SOCRATES: Or on a voyage?
ALCIBIADES: No.
SOCRATES: Or reaping the harvest?
ALCIBIADES: No.
SOCRATES: When they are doing something or nothing?
ALCIBIADES: When they are doing something, I should say.
SOCRATES: I wish that you would explain to me what this something is.
ALCIBIADES: When they are having dealings with one another, and using one another's services, as we citizens do in our daily life.
SOCRATES: Those of whom you speak are ruling over men who are using the services of other men?
ALCIBIADES: Yes.
SOCRATES: Are they ruling over the signal-men who give the time to the rowers?
ALCIBIADES: No; they are not.
SOCRATES: That would be the office of the pilot?
ALCIBIADES: Yes.
SOCRATES: But, perhaps you mean that they rule over flute-players, who lead the singers and use the services of the dancers?
ALCIBIADES: Certainly not.
SOCRATES: That would be the business of the teacher of the chorus?
ALCIBIADES: Yes.
SOCRATES: Then what is the meaning of being able to rule over men who use other men?
ALCIBIADES: I mean that they rule over men who have common rights of citizenship, and dealings with one another.
SOCRATES: And what sort of an art is this? Suppose that I ask you again, as I did just now, What art makes men know how to rule over their fellow-sailors,--

how would you answer?

ALCIBIADES: The art of the pilot.

SOCRATES: And, if I may recur to another old instance, what art enables them to rule over their fellow-singers?

ALCIBIADES: The art of the teacher of the chorus, which you were just now mentioning.

SOCRATES: And what do you call the art of fellow-citizens?

ALCIBIADES: I should say, good counsel, Socrates.

SOCRATES: And is the art of the pilot evil counsel?

ALCIBIADES: No.

SOCRATES: But good counsel?

ALCIBIADES: Yes, that is what I should say,--good counsel, of which the aim is the preservation of the voyagers.

SOCRATES: True. And what is the aim of that other good counsel of which you speak?

ALCIBIADES: The aim is the better order and preservation of the city.

SOCRATES: And what is that of which the absence or presence improves and preserves the order of the city? Suppose you were to ask me, what is that of which the presence or absence improves or preserves the order of the body? I should reply, the presence of health and the absence of disease. You would say the same?

ALCIBIADES: Yes.

SOCRATES: And if you were to ask me the same question about the eyes, I should reply in the same way, 'the presence of sight and the absence of blindness;' or about the ears, I should reply, that they were improved and were in better case, when deafness was absent, and hearing was present in them.

ALCIBIADES: True.

SOCRATES: And what would you say of a state? What is that by the presence or absence of which the state is improved and better managed and ordered?

ALCIBIADES: I should say, Socrates:--the presence of friendship and the absence of hatred and division.

SOCRATES: And do you mean by friendship agreement or disagreement?

ALCIBIADES: Agreement.

SOCRATES: What art makes cities agree about numbers?

ALCIBIADES: Arithmetic.
SOCRATES: And private individuals?
ALCIBIADES: The same.
SOCRATES: And what art makes each individual agree with himself?
ALCIBIADES: The same.
SOCRATES: And what art makes each of us agree with himself about the comparative length of the span and of the cubit? Does not the art of measure?
ALCIBIADES: Yes.
SOCRATES: Individuals are agreed with one another about this; and states, equally?
ALCIBIADES: Yes.
SOCRATES: And the same holds of the balance?
ALCIBIADES: True.
SOCRATES: But what is the other agreement of which you speak, and about what? what art can give that agreement? And does that which gives it to the state give it also to the individual, so as to make him consistent with himself and with another?
ALCIBIADES: I should suppose so.
SOCRATES: But what is the nature of the agreement?--answer, and faint not.
ALCIBIADES: I mean to say that there should be such friendship and agreement as exists between an affectionate father and mother and their son, or between brothers, or between husband and wife.
SOCRATES: But can a man, Alcibiades, agree with a woman about the spinning of wool, which she understands and he does not?
ALCIBIADES: No, truly.
SOCRATES: Nor has he any need, for spinning is a female accomplishment.
ALCIBIADES: Yes.
SOCRATES: And would a woman agree with a man about the science of arms, which she has never learned?
ALCIBIADES: Certainly not.
SOCRATES: I suppose that the use of arms would be regarded by you as a male accomplishment?
ALCIBIADES: It would.

SOCRATES: Then, upon your view, women and men have two sorts of knowledge?

ALCIBIADES: Certainly.

SOCRATES: Then in their knowledge there is no agreement of women and men?

ALCIBIADES: There is not.

SOCRATES: Nor can there be friendship, if friendship is agreement?

ALCIBIADES: Plainly not.

SOCRATES: Then women are not loved by men when they do their own work?

ALCIBIADES: I suppose not.

SOCRATES: Nor men by women when they do their own work?

ALCIBIADES: No.

SOCRATES: Nor are states well administered, when individuals do their own work?

ALCIBIADES: I should rather think, Socrates, that the reverse is the truth. (Compare Republic.)

SOCRATES: What! do you mean to say that states are well administered when friendship is absent, the presence of which, as we were saying, alone secures their good order?

ALCIBIADES: But I should say that there is friendship among them, for this very reason, that the two parties respectively do their own work.

SOCRATES: That was not what you were saying before; and what do you mean now by affirming that friendship exists when there is no agreement? How can there be agreement about matters which the one party knows, and of which the other is in ignorance?

ALCIBIADES: Impossible.

SOCRATES: And when individuals are doing their own work, are they doing what is just or unjust?

ALCIBIADES: What is just, certainly.

SOCRATES: And when individuals do what is just in the state, is there no friendship among them?

ALCIBIADES: I suppose that there must be, Socrates.

SOCRATES: Then what do you mean by this friendship or agreement about which we must be wise and discreet in order that we may be good men? I cannot make out where it exists or among whom; according to you, the same persons may sometimes have it, and sometimes not.

ALCIBIADES: But, indeed, Socrates, I do not know what I am saying; and I have long been, unconsciously to myself, in a most disgraceful state.

SOCRATES: Nevertheless, cheer up; at fifty, if you had discovered your deficiency, you would have been too old, and the time for taking care of yourself would have passed away, but yours is just the age at which the discovery should be made.

ALCIBIADES: And what should he do, Socrates, who would make the discovery?

SOCRATES: Answer questions, Alcibiades; and that is a process which, by the grace of God, if I may put any faith in my oracle, will be very improving to both of us.

ALCIBIADES: If I can be improved by answering, I will answer.

SOCRATES: And first of all, that we may not peradventure be deceived by appearances, fancying, perhaps, that we are taking care of ourselves when we are not, what is the meaning of a man taking care of himself? and when does he take care? Does he take care of himself when he takes care of what belongs to him?

ALCIBIADES: I should think so.

SOCRATES: When does a man take care of his feet? Does he not take care of them when he takes care of that which belongs to his feet?

ALCIBIADES: I do not understand.

SOCRATES: Let me take the hand as an illustration; does not a ring belong to the finger, and to the finger only?

ALCIBIADES: Yes.

SOCRATES: And the shoe in like manner to the foot?

ALCIBIADES: Yes.

SOCRATES: And when we take care of our shoes, do we not take care of our feet?

ALCIBIADES: I do not comprehend, Socrates.

SOCRATES: But you would admit, Alcibiades, that to take proper care of a thing is a correct expression?

ALCIBIADES: Yes.

SOCRATES: And taking proper care means improving?

ALCIBIADES: Yes.

SOCRATES: And what is the art which improves our shoes?

ALCIBIADES: Shoemaking.

SOCRATES: Then by shoemaking we take care of our shoes?

ALCIBIADES: Yes.

SOCRATES: And do we by shoemaking take care of our feet, or by some other art which improves the feet?

ALCIBIADES: By some other art.

SOCRATES: And the same art improves the feet which improves the rest of the body?

ALCIBIADES: Very true.

SOCRATES: Which is gymnastic?

ALCIBIADES: Certainly.

SOCRATES: Then by gymnastic we take care of our feet, and by shoemaking of that which belongs to our feet?

ALCIBIADES: Very true.

SOCRATES: And by gymnastic we take care of our hands, and by the art of graving rings of that which belongs to our hands?

ALCIBIADES: Yes.

SOCRATES: And by gymnastic we take care of the body, and by the art of weaving and the other arts we take care of the things of the body?

ALCIBIADES: Clearly.

SOCRATES: Then the art which takes care of each thing is different from that which takes care of the belongings of each thing?

ALCIBIADES: True.

SOCRATES: Then in taking care of what belongs to you, you do not take care of yourself?

ALCIBIADES: Certainly not.

SOCRATES: For the art which takes care of our belongings appears not to be the same as that which takes care of ourselves?

ALCIBIADES: Clearly not.

SOCRATES: And now let me ask you what is the art with which we take care of ourselves?

ALCIBIADES: I cannot say.

SOCRATES: At any rate, thus much has been admitted, that the art is not one which makes any of our possessions, but which makes ourselves better?

ALCIBIADES: True.

SOCRATES: But should we ever have known what art makes a shoe better, if we did not know a shoe?

ALCIBIADES: Impossible.

SOCRATES: Nor should we know what art makes a ring better, if we did not know a ring?

ALCIBIADES: That is true.

SOCRATES: And can we ever know what art makes a man better, if we do not know what we are ourselves?

ALCIBIADES: Impossible.

SOCRATES: And is self-knowledge such an easy thing, and was he to be lightly esteemed who inscribed the text on the temple at Delphi? Or is self-knowledge a difficult thing, which few are able to attain?

ALCIBIADES: At times I fancy, Socrates, that anybody can know himself; at other times the task appears to be very difficult.

SOCRATES: But whether easy or difficult, Alcibiades, still there is no other way; knowing what we are, we shall know how to take care of ourselves, and if we are ignorant we shall not know.

ALCIBIADES: That is true.

SOCRATES: Well, then, let us see in what way the self-existent can be discovered by us; that will give us a chance of discovering our own existence, which otherwise we can never know.

ALCIBIADES: You say truly.

SOCRATES: Come, now, I beseech you, tell me with whom you are conversing?--with whom but with me?

ALCIBIADES: Yes.

SOCRATES: As I am, with you?

ALCIBIADES: Yes.

SOCRATES: That is to say, I, Socrates, am talking?
ALCIBIADES: Yes.
SOCRATES: And Alcibiades is my hearer?
ALCIBIADES: Yes.
SOCRATES: And I in talking use words?
ALCIBIADES: Certainly.
SOCRATES: And talking and using words have, I suppose, the same meaning?
ALCIBIADES: To be sure.
SOCRATES: And the user is not the same as the thing which he uses?
ALCIBIADES: What do you mean?
SOCRATES: I will explain; the shoemaker, for example, uses a square tool, and a circular tool, and other tools for cutting?
ALCIBIADES: Yes.
SOCRATES: But the tool is not the same as the cutter and user of the tool?
ALCIBIADES: Of course not.
SOCRATES: And in the same way the instrument of the harper is to be distinguished from the harper himself?
ALCIBIADES: It is.
SOCRATES: Now the question which I asked was whether you conceive the user to be always different from that which he uses?
ALCIBIADES: I do.
SOCRATES: Then what shall we say of the shoemaker? Does he cut with his tools only or with his hands?
ALCIBIADES: With his hands as well.
SOCRATES: He uses his hands too?
ALCIBIADES: Yes.
SOCRATES: And does he use his eyes in cutting leather?
ALCIBIADES: He does.
SOCRATES: And we admit that the user is not the same with the things which he uses?
ALCIBIADES: Yes.
SOCRATES: Then the shoemaker and the harper are to be distinguished from the hands and feet which they use?

ALCIBIADES: Clearly.
SOCRATES: And does not a man use the whole body?
ALCIBIADES: Certainly.
SOCRATES: And that which uses is different from that which is used?
ALCIBIADES: True.
SOCRATES: Then a man is not the same as his own body?
ALCIBIADES: That is the inference.
SOCRATES: What is he, then?
ALCIBIADES: I cannot say.
SOCRATES: Nay, you can say that he is the user of the body.
ALCIBIADES: Yes.
SOCRATES: And the user of the body is the soul?
ALCIBIADES: Yes, the soul.
SOCRATES: And the soul rules?
ALCIBIADES: Yes.
SOCRATES: Let me make an assertion which will, I think, be universally admitted.
ALCIBIADES: What is it?
SOCRATES: That man is one of three things.
ALCIBIADES: What are they?
SOCRATES: Soul, body, or both together forming a whole.
ALCIBIADES: Certainly.
SOCRATES: But did we not say that the actual ruling principle of the body is man?
ALCIBIADES: Yes, we did.
SOCRATES: And does the body rule over itself?
ALCIBIADES: Certainly not.
SOCRATES: It is subject, as we were saying?
ALCIBIADES: Yes.
SOCRATES: Then that is not the principle which we are seeking?
ALCIBIADES: It would seem not.
SOCRATES: But may we say that the union of the two rules over the body, and consequently that this is man?

ALCIBIADES: Very likely.

SOCRATES: The most unlikely of all things; for if one of the members is subject, the two united cannot possibly rule.

ALCIBIADES: True.

SOCRATES: But since neither the body, nor the union of the two, is man, either man has no real existence, or the soul is man?

ALCIBIADES: Just so.

SOCRATES: Is anything more required to prove that the soul is man?

ALCIBIADES: Certainly not; the proof is, I think, quite sufficient.

SOCRATES: And if the proof, although not perfect, be sufficient, we shall be satisfied;--more precise proof will be supplied when we have discovered that which we were led to omit, from a fear that the enquiry would be too much protracted.

ALCIBIADES: What was that?

SOCRATES: What I meant, when I said that absolute existence must be first considered; but now, instead of absolute existence, we have been considering the nature of individual existence, and this may, perhaps, be sufficient; for surely there is nothing which may be called more properly ourselves than the soul?

ALCIBIADES: There is nothing.

SOCRATES: Then we may truly conceive that you and I are conversing with one another, soul to soul?

ALCIBIADES: Very true.

SOCRATES: And that is just what I was saying before--that I, Socrates, am not arguing or talking with the face of Alcibiades, but with the real Alcibiades; or in other words, with his soul.

ALCIBIADES: True.

SOCRATES: Then he who bids a man know himself, would have him know his soul?

ALCIBIADES: That appears to be true.

SOCRATES: He whose knowledge only extends to the body, knows the things of a man, and not the man himself?

ALCIBIADES: That is true.

SOCRATES: Then neither the physician regarded as a physician, nor the trainer regarded as a trainer, knows himself?

ALCIBIADES: He does not.

SOCRATES: The husbandmen and the other craftsmen are very far from knowing themselves, for they would seem not even to know their own belongings? When regarded in relation to the arts which they practise they are even further removed from self-knowledge, for they only know the belongings of the body, which minister to the body.

ALCIBIADES: That is true.

SOCRATES: Then if temperance is the knowledge of self, in respect of his art none of them is temperate?

ALCIBIADES: I agree.

SOCRATES: And this is the reason why their arts are accounted vulgar, and are not such as a good man would practise?

ALCIBIADES: Quite true.

SOCRATES: Again, he who cherishes his body cherishes not himself, but what belongs to him?

ALCIBIADES: That is true.

SOCRATES: But he who cherishes his money, cherishes neither himself nor his belongings, but is in a stage yet further removed from himself?

ALCIBIADES: I agree.

SOCRATES: Then the money-maker has really ceased to be occupied with his own concerns?

ALCIBIADES: True.

SOCRATES: And if any one has fallen in love with the person of Alcibiades, he loves not Alcibiades, but the belongings of Alcibiades?

ALCIBIADES: True.

SOCRATES: But he who loves your soul is the true lover?

ALCIBIADES: That is the necessary inference.

SOCRATES: The lover of the body goes away when the flower of youth fades?

ALCIBIADES: True.

SOCRATES: But he who loves the soul goes not away, as long as the soul follows after virtue?

ALCIBIADES: Yes.

SOCRATES: And I am the lover who goes not away, but remains with you, when you are no longer young and the rest are gone?

ALCIBIADES: Yes, Socrates; and therein you do well, and I hope that you will remain.

SOCRATES: Then you must try to look your best.

ALCIBIADES: I will.

SOCRATES: The fact is, that there is only one lover of Alcibiades the son of Cleinias; there neither is nor ever has been seemingly any other; and he is his darling,--Socrates, the son of Sophroniscus and Phaenarete.

ALCIBIADES: True.

SOCRATES: And did you not say, that if I had not spoken first, you were on the point of coming to me, and enquiring why I only remained?

ALCIBIADES: That is true.

SOCRATES: The reason was that I loved you for your own sake, whereas other men love what belongs to you; and your beauty, which is not you, is fading away, just as your true self is beginning to bloom. And I will never desert you, if you are not spoiled and deformed by the Athenian people; for the danger which I most fear is that you will become a lover of the people and will be spoiled by them. Many a noble Athenian has been ruined in this way. For the demus of the great-hearted Erechteus is of a fair countenance, but you should see him naked; wherefore observe the caution which I give you.

ALCIBIADES: What caution?

SOCRATES: Practise yourself, sweet friend, in learning what you ought to know, before you enter on politics; and then you will have an antidote which will keep you out of harm's way.

ALCIBIADES: Good advice, Socrates, but I wish that you would explain to me in what way I am to take care of myself.

SOCRATES: Have we not made an advance? for we are at any rate tolerably well agreed as to what we are, and there is no longer any danger, as we once feared, that we might be taking care not of ourselves, but of something which is not ourselves.

ALCIBIADES: That is true.

SOCRATES: And the next step will be to take care of the soul, and look to that?

ALCIBIADES: Certainly.

SOCRATES: Leaving the care of our bodies and of our properties to others?

ALCIBIADES: Very good.

SOCRATES: But how can we have a perfect knowledge of the things of the soul?--For if we know them, then I suppose we shall know ourselves. Can we really be ignorant of the excellent meaning of the Delphian inscription, of which we were just now speaking?

ALCIBIADES: What have you in your thoughts, Socrates?

SOCRATES: I will tell you what I suspect to be the meaning and lesson of that inscription. Let me take an illustration from sight, which I imagine to be the only one suitable to my purpose.

ALCIBIADES: What do you mean?

SOCRATES: Consider; if some one were to say to the eye, 'See thyself,' as you might say to a man, 'Know thyself,' what is the nature and meaning of this precept? Would not his meaning be:--That the eye should look at that in which it would see itself?

ALCIBIADES: Clearly.

SOCRATES: And what are the objects in looking at which we see ourselves?

ALCIBIADES: Clearly, Socrates, in looking at mirrors and the like.

SOCRATES: Very true; and is there not something of the nature of a mirror in our own eyes?

ALCIBIADES: Certainly.

SOCRATES: Did you ever observe that the face of the person looking into the eye of another is reflected as in a mirror; and in the visual organ which is over against him, and which is called the pupil, there is a sort of image of the person looking?

ALCIBIADES: That is quite true.

SOCRATES: Then the eye, looking at another eye, and at that in the eye which is most perfect, and which is the instrument of vision, will there see itself?

ALCIBIADES: That is evident.

SOCRATES: But looking at anything else either in man or in the world, and not to what resembles this, it will not see itself?

ALCIBIADES: Very true.

SOCRATES: Then if the eye is to see itself, it must look at the eye, and at that part of the eye where sight which is the virtue of the eye resides?

ALCIBIADES: True.

SOCRATES: And if the soul, my dear Alcibiades, is ever to know herself, must she not look at the soul; and especially at that part of the soul in which her virtue resides, and to any other which is like this?

ALCIBIADES: I agree, Socrates.

SOCRATES: And do we know of any part of our souls more divine than that which has to do with wisdom and knowledge?

ALCIBIADES: There is none.

SOCRATES: Then this is that part of the soul which resembles the divine; and he who looks at this and at the whole class of things divine, will be most likely to know himself?

ALCIBIADES: Clearly.

SOCRATES: And self-knowledge we agree to be wisdom?

ALCIBIADES: True.

SOCRATES: But if we have no self-knowledge and no wisdom, can we ever know our own good and evil?

ALCIBIADES: How can we, Socrates?

SOCRATES: You mean, that if you did not know Alcibiades, there would be no possibility of your knowing that what belonged to Alcibiades was really his?

ALCIBIADES: It would be quite impossible.

SOCRATES: Nor should we know that we were the persons to whom anything belonged, if we did not know ourselves?

ALCIBIADES: How could we?

SOCRATES: And if we did not know our own belongings, neither should we know the belongings of our belongings?

ALCIBIADES: Clearly not.

SOCRATES: Then we were not altogether right in acknowledging just now that a man may know what belongs to him and yet not know himself; nay, rather he cannot even know the belongings of his belongings; for the discernment of the things of self, and of the things which belong to the things of self, appear all to be the business of the same man, and of the same art.

ALCIBIADES: So much may be supposed.

SOCRATES: And he who knows not the things which belong to himself, will in like manner be ignorant of the things which belong to others?

ALCIBIADES: Very true.

SOCRATES: And if he knows not the affairs of others, he will not know the affairs of states?

ALCIBIADES: Certainly not.

SOCRATES: Then such a man can never be a statesman?

ALCIBIADES: He cannot.

SOCRATES: Nor an economist?

ALCIBIADES: He cannot.

SOCRATES: He will not know what he is doing?

ALCIBIADES: He will not.

SOCRATES: And will not he who is ignorant fall into error?

ALCIBIADES: Assuredly.

SOCRATES: And if he falls into error will he not fail both in his public and private capacity?

ALCIBIADES: Yes, indeed.

SOCRATES: And failing, will he not be miserable?

ALCIBIADES: Very.

SOCRATES: And what will become of those for whom he is acting?

ALCIBIADES: They will be miserable also.

SOCRATES: Then he who is not wise and good cannot be happy?

ALCIBIADES: He cannot.

SOCRATES: The bad, then, are miserable?

ALCIBIADES: Yes, very.

SOCRATES: And if so, not he who has riches, but he who has wisdom, is delivered from his misery?

ALCIBIADES: Clearly.

SOCRATES: Cities, then, if they are to be happy, do not want walls, or triremes, or docks, or numbers, or size, Alcibiades, without virtue? (Compare Arist. Pol.)

ALCIBIADES: Indeed they do not.

SOCRATES: And you must give the citizens virtue, if you mean to administer their affairs rightly or nobly?

ALCIBIADES: Certainly.

SOCRATES: But can a man give that which he has not?

ALCIBIADES: Impossible.

SOCRATES: Then you or any one who means to govern and superintend, not only himself and the things of himself, but the state and the things of the state, must in the first place acquire virtue.

ALCIBIADES: That is true.

SOCRATES: You have not therefore to obtain power or authority, in order to enable you to do what you wish for yourself and the state, but justice and wisdom.

ALCIBIADES: Clearly.

SOCRATES: You and the state, if you act wisely and justly, will act according to the will of God?

ALCIBIADES: Certainly.

SOCRATES: As I was saying before, you will look only at what is bright and divine, and act with a view to them?

ALCIBIADES: Yes.

SOCRATES: In that mirror you will see and know yourselves and your own good?

ALCIBIADES: Yes.

SOCRATES: And so you will act rightly and well?

ALCIBIADES: Yes.

SOCRATES: In which case, I will be security for your happiness.

ALCIBIADES: I accept the security.

SOCRATES: But if you act unrighteously, your eye will turn to the dark and godless, and being in darkness and ignorance of yourselves, you will probably do deeds of darkness.

ALCIBIADES: Very possibly.

SOCRATES: For if a man, my dear Alcibiades, has the power to do what he likes, but has no understanding, what is likely to be the result, either to him as an individual or to the state--for example, if he be sick and is able to do what he likes, not having the mind of a physician--having moreover tyrannical power, and no one daring to reprove him, what will happen to him? Will he not be likely to have his constitution ruined?

ALCIBIADES: That is true.

SOCRATES: Or again, in a ship, if a man having the power to do what he likes, has no intelligence or skill in navigation, do you see what will happen to him and to his fellow-sailors?

ALCIBIADES: Yes; I see that they will all perish.

SOCRATES: And in like manner, in a state, and where there is any power and authority which is wanting in virtue, will not misfortune, in like manner, ensue?

ALCIBIADES: Certainly.

SOCRATES: Not tyrannical power, then, my good Alcibiades, should be the aim either of individuals or states, if they would be happy, but virtue.

ALCIBIADES: That is true.

SOCRATES: And before they have virtue, to be commanded by a superior is better for men as well as for children? (Compare Arist. Pol.)

ALCIBIADES: That is evident.

SOCRATES: And that which is better is also nobler?

ALCIBIADES: True.

SOCRATES: And what is nobler is more becoming?

ALCIBIADES: Certainly.

SOCRATES: Then to the bad man slavery is more becoming, because better?

ALCIBIADES: True.

SOCRATES: Then vice is only suited to a slave?

ALCIBIADES: Yes.

SOCRATES: And virtue to a freeman?

ALCIBIADES: Yes.

SOCRATES: And, O my friend, is not the condition of a slave to be avoided?

ALCIBIADES: Certainly, Socrates.

SOCRATES: And are you now conscious of your own state? And do you know whether you are a freeman or not?

ALCIBIADES: I think that I am very conscious indeed of my own state.

SOCRATES: And do you know how to escape out of a state which I do not even like to name to my beauty?

ALCIBIADES: Yes, I do.

SOCRATES: How?

ALCIBIADES: By your help, Socrates.

SOCRATES: That is not well said, Alcibiades.

ALCIBIADES: What ought I to have said?

SOCRATES: By the help of God.

ALCIBIADES: I agree; and I further say, that our relations are likely to be reversed. From this day forward, I must and will follow you as you have followed me; I will be the disciple, and you shall be my master.

SOCRATES: O that is rare! My love breeds another love: and so like the stork I shall be cherished by the bird whom I have hatched.

ALCIBIADES: Strange, but true; and henceforward I shall begin to think about justice.

SOCRATES: And I hope that you will persist; although I have fears, not because I doubt you; but I see the power of the state, which may be too much for both of us.

www.bookjungle.com email: sales@bookjungle.com fax: 630-214-0564 mail: Book Jungle PO Box 2226 Champaign, IL 61825

The Codes Of Hammurabi And Moses
W. W. Davies

QTY

The discovery of the Hammurabi Code is one of the greatest achievements of archaeology, and is of paramount interest, not only to the student of the Bible, but also to all those interested in ancient history...

Religion   ISBN: *1-59462-338-4*   **Pages:132**
MSRP $12.95

The Theory of Moral Sentiments
Adam Smith

QTY

This work from 1749. contains original theories of conscience amd moral judgment and it is the foundation for systemof morals.

Philosophy   ISBN: *1-59462-777-0*   **Pages:536**
MSRP $19.95

Jessica's First Prayer
Hesba Stretton

QTY

In a screened and secluded corner of one of the many railway-bridges which span the streets of London there could be seen a few years ago, from five o'clock every morning until half past eight, a tidily set-out coffee-stall, consisting of a trestle and board, upon which stood two large tin cans, with a small fire of charcoal burning under each so as to keep the coffee boiling during the early hours of the morning when the work-people were thronging into the city on their way to their daily toil...

Childrens   ISBN: *1-59462-373-2*   **Pages:84**
MSRP $9.95

My Life and Work
Henry Ford

QTY

Henry Ford revolutionized the world with his implementation of mass production for the Model T automobile. Gain valuable business insight into his life and work with his own auto-biography... "We have only started on our development of our country we have not as yet, with all our talk of wonderful progress, done more than scratch the surface. The progress has been wonderful enough but..."

Biographies/   ISBN: *1-59462-198-5*   **Pages:300**
MSRP $21.95

www.bookjungle.com *email: sales@bookjungle.com fax: 630-214-0564 mail: Book Jungle PO Box 2226 Champaign, IL 61825*

The Art of Cross-Examination
Francis Wellman

QTY

I presume it is the experience of every author, after his first book is published upon an important subject, to be almost overwhelmed with a wealth of ideas and illustrations which could readily have been included in his book, and which to his own mind, at least, seem to make a second edition inevitable. Such certainly was the case with me; and when the first edition had reached its sixth impression in five months, I rejoiced to learn that it seemed to my publishers that the book had met with a sufficiently favorable reception to justify a second and considerably enlarged edition. ..

Reference   ISBN: *1-59462-647-2*   Pages:412   *MSRP $19.95*

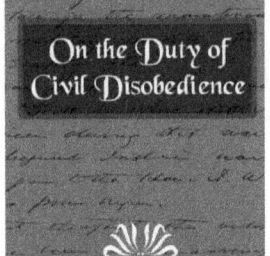

On the Duty of Civil Disobedience
Henry David Thoreau

QTY

Thoreau wrote his famous essay, On the Duty of Civil Disobedience, as a protest against an unjust but popular war and the immoral but popular institution of slave-owning. He did more than write—he declined to pay his taxes, and was hauled off to gaol in consequence. Who can say how much this refusal of his hastened the end of the war and of slavery ?

Law   ISBN: *1-59462-747-9*   Pages:48   *MSRP $7.45*

Dream Psychology Psychoanalysis for Beginners
Sigmund Freud

QTY

Sigmund Freud, born Sigismund Schlomo Freud (May 6, 1856 - September 23, 1939), was a Jewish-Austrian neurologist and psychiatrist who co-founded the psychoanalytic school of psychology. Freud is best known for his theories of the unconscious mind, especially involving the mechanism of repression; his redefinition of sexual desire as mobile and directed towards a wide variety of objects; and his therapeutic techniques, especially his understanding of transference in the therapeutic relationship and the presumed value of dreams as sources of insight into unconscious desires.

Psychology   ISBN: *1-59462-905-6*   Pages:196   *MSRP $15.45*

The Miracle of Right Thought
Orison Swett Marden

QTY

Believe with all of your heart that you will do what you were made to do. When the mind has once formed the habit of holding cheerful, happy, prosperous pictures, it will not be easy to form the opposite habit. It does not matter how improbable or how far away this realization may see, or how dark the prospects may be, if we visualize them as best we can, as vividly as possible, hold tenaciously to them and vigorously struggle to attain them, they will gradually become actualized, realized in the life. But a desire, a longing without endeavor, a yearning abandoned or held indifferently will vanish without realization.

Self Help   ISBN: *1-59462-644-8*   Pages:360   *MSRP $25.45*

www.bookjungle.com email: sales@bookjungle.com fax: 630-214-0564 mail: Book Jungle PO Box 2226 Champaign, IL 61825

QTY

	Title	ISBN	Price
☐	**The Rosicrucian Cosmo-Conception Mystic Christianity** by *Max Heindel*	ISBN: *1-59462-188-8*	**$38.95**

The Rosicrucian Cosmo-conception is not dogmatic, neither does it appeal to any other authority than the reason of the student. It is: not controversial, but is: sent forth in the, hope that it may help to clear...
New Age/Religion Pages 646

☐ **Abandonment To Divine Providence** by *Jean-Pierre de Caussade* ISBN: *1-59462-228-0* **$25.95**
"The Rev. Jean Pierre de Caussade was one of the most remarkable spiritual writers of the Society of Jesus in France in the 18th Century. His death took place at Toulouse in 1751. His works have gone through many editions and have been republished..."
Inspirational/Religion Pages 400

☐ **Mental Chemistry** by *Charles Haanel* ISBN: *1-59462-192-6* **$23.95**
Mental Chemistry allows the change of material conditions by combining and appropriately utilizing the power of the mind. Much like applied chemistry creates something new and unique out of careful combinations of chemicals the mastery of mental chemistry...
New Age Pages 354

☐ **The Letters of Robert Browning and Elizabeth Barret Barrett 1845-1846 vol II** ISBN: *1-59462-193-4* **$35.95**
by *Robert Browning and Elizabeth Barrett*
Biographies Pages 596

☐ **Gleanings In Genesis (volume I)** by *Arthur W. Pink* ISBN: *1-59462-130-6* **$27.45**
Appropriately has Genesis been termed "the seed plot of the Bible" for in it we have, in germ form, almost all of the great doctrines which are afterwards fully developed in the books of Scripture which follow...
Religion/Inspirational Pages 420

☐ **The Master Key** by *L. W. de Laurence* ISBN: *1-59462-001-6* **$30.95**
In no branch of human knowledge has there been a more lively increase of the spirit of research during the past few years than in the study of Psychology, Concentration and Mental Discipline. The requests for authentic lessons in Thought Control, Mental Discipline and...
New Age/Business Pages 422

☐ **The Lesser Key Of Solomon Goetia** by *L. W. de Laurence* ISBN: *1-59462-092-X* **$9.95**
This translation of the first book of the "Lernegton" which is now for the first time made accessible to students of Talismanic Magic was done, after careful collation and edition, from numerous Ancient Manuscripts in Hebrew, Latin, and French...
New Age/Occult Pages 92

☐ **Rubaiyat Of Omar Khayyam** by *Edward Fitzgerald* ISBN:*1-59462-332-5* **$13.95**
Edward Fitzgerald, whom the world has already learned, in spite of his own efforts to remain within the shadow of anonymity, to look upon as one of the rarest poets of the century, was born at Bredfield, in Suffolk, on the 31st of March, 1809. He was the third son of John Purcell...
Music Pages 172

☐ **Ancient Law** by *Henry Maine* ISBN: *1-59462-128-4* **$29.95**
The chief object of the following pages is to indicate some of the earliest ideas of mankind, as they are reflected in Ancient Law, and to point out the relation of those ideas to modern thought.
Religion/History Pages 452

☐ **Far-Away Stories** by *William J. Locke* ISBN: *1-59462-129-2* **$19.45**
"Good wine needs no bush, but a collection of mixed vintages does. And this book is just such a collection. Some of the stories I do not want to remain buried for ever in the museum files of dead magazine-numbers an author's not unpardonable vanity..."
Fiction Pages 272

☐ **Life of David Crockett** by *David Crockett* ISBN: *1-59462-250-7* **$27.45**
"Colonel David Crockett was one of the most remarkable men of the times in which he lived. Born in humble life, but gifted with a strong will, an indomitable courage, and unremitting perseverance...
Biographies/New Age Pages 424

☐ **Lip-Reading** by *Edward Nitchie* ISBN: *1-59462-206-X* **$25.95**
Edward B. Nitchie, founder of the New York School for the Hard of Hearing, now the Nitchie School of Lip-Reading, Inc, wrote "LIP-READING Principles and Practice". The development and perfecting of this meritorious work on lip-reading was an undertaking...
How-to Pages 400

☐ **A Handbook of Suggestive Therapeutics, Applied Hypnotism, Psychic Science** ISBN: *1-59462-214-0* **$24.95**
by *Henry Munro*
Health/New Age/Health/Self-help Pages 376

☐ **A Doll's House: and Two Other Plays** by *Henrik Ibsen* ISBN: *1-59462-112-8* **$19.95**
Henrik Ibsen created this classic when in revolutionary 1848 Rome. Introducing some striking concepts in playwriting for the realist genre, this play has been studied the world over.
Fiction/Classics/Plays 308

☐ **The Light of Asia** by *sir Edwin Arnold* ISBN: *1-59462-204-3* **$13.95**
In this poetic masterpiece, Edwin Arnold describes the life and teachings of Buddha. The man who was to become known as Buddha to the world was born as Prince Gautama of India but he rejected the worldly riches and abandoned the reigns of power when...
Religion/History/Biographies Pages 170

☐ **The Complete Works of Guy de Maupassant** by *Guy de Maupassant* ISBN: *1-59462-157-8* **$16.95**
"For days and days, nights and nights, I had dreamed of that first kiss which was to consecrate our engagement, and I knew not on what spot I should put my lips..."
Fiction/Classics Pages 240

☐ **The Art of Cross-Examination** by *Francis L. Wellman* ISBN: *1-59462-309-0* **$26.95**
Written by a renowned trial lawyer, Wellman imparts his experience and uses case studies to explain how to use psychology to extract desired information through questioning.
How-to/Science/Reference Pages 408

☐ **Answered or Unanswered?** by *Louisa Vaughan* ISBN: *1-59462-248-5* **$10.95**
Miracles of Faith in China
Religion Pages 112

☐ **The Edinburgh Lectures on Mental Science (1909)** by *Thomas* ISBN: *1-59462-008-3* **$11.95**
This book contains the substance of a course of lectures recently given by the writer in the Queen Street Hall, Edinburgh. Its purpose is to indicate the Natural Principles governing the relation between Mental Action and Material Conditions...
New Age/Psychology Pages 148

☐ **Ayesha** by *H. Rider Haggard* ISBN: *1-59462-301-5* **$24.95**
Verily and indeed it is the unexpected that happens! Probably if there was one person upon the earth from whom the Editor of this, and of a certain previous history, did not expect to hear again...
Classics Pages 380

☐ **Ayala's Angel** by *Anthony Trollope* ISBN: *1-59462-352-X* **$29.95**
The two girls were both pretty, but Lucy who was twenty-one who supposed to be simple and comparatively unattractive, whereas Ayala was credited, as her Bombwhat romantic name might show, with poetic charm and a taste for romance. Ayala when her father died was nineteen...
Fiction Pages 484

☐ **The American Commonwealth** by *James Bryce* ISBN: *1-59462-286-8* **$34.45**
An interpretation of American democratic political theory. It examines political mechanics and society from the perspective of Scotsman James Bryce
Politics Pages 572

☐ **Stories of the Pilgrims** by *Margaret P. Pumphrey* ISBN: *1-59462-116-0* **$17.95**
This book explores pilgrims religious oppression in England as well as their escape to Holland and eventual crossing to America on the Mayflower, and their early days in New England...
History Pages 268

www.bookjungle.com email: sales@bookjungle.com fax: 630-214-0564 mail: Book Jungle PO Box 2226 Champaign, IL 61825

QTY

The Fasting Cure by **Sinclair Upton** ISBN: *1-59462-222-1* **$13.95**
In the Cosmopolitan Magazine for May, 1910, and in the Contemporary Review (London) for April, 1910, I published an article dealing with my experiences in fasting. I have written a great many magazine articles, but never one which attracted so much attention... New Age/Self Help/Health Pages 164

Hebrew Astrology by **Sepharial** ISBN: *1-59462-308-2* **$13.45**
In these days of advanced thinking it is a matter of common observation that we have left many of the old landmarks behind and that we are now pressing forward to greater heights and to a wider horizon than that which represented the mind-content of our progenitors... Astrology Pages 144

Thought Vibration or The Law of Attraction in the Thought World ISBN: *1-59462-127-6* **$12.95**
by **William Walker Atkinson** Psychology/Religion Pages 144

Optimism by **Helen Keller** ISBN: *1-59462-108-X* **$15.95**
Helen Keller was blind, deaf, and mute since 19 months old, yet famously learned how to overcome these handicaps, communicate with the world, and spread her lectures promoting optimism. An inspiring read for everyone... Biographies/Inspirational Pages 84

Sara Crewe by **Frances Burnett** ISBN: *1-59462-360-0* **$9.45**
In the first place, Miss Minchin lived in London. Her home was a large, dull, tall one, in a large, dull square, where all the houses were alike, and all the sparrows were alike, and where all the door-knockers made the same heavy sound... Childrens/Classic Pages 88

The Autobiography of Benjamin Franklin by **Benjamin Franklin** ISBN: *1-59462-135-7* **$24.95**
The Autobiography of Benjamin Franklin has probably been more extensively read than any other American historical work, and no other book of its kind has had such ups and downs of fortune. Franklin lived for many years in England, where he was agent... Biographies/History Pages 332

| Name |
| Email |
| Telephone |
| Address |
| |
| City, State ZIP |

☐ Credit Card   ☐ Check / Money Order

| Credit Card Number |
| Expiration Date |
| Signature |

Please Mail to: Book Jungle
PO Box 2226
Champaign, IL 61825
or Fax to: 630-214-0564

ORDERING INFORMATION

web: *www.bookjungle.com*
email: *sales@bookjungle.com*
fax: 630-214-0564
mail: *Book Jungle PO Box 2226 Champaign, IL 61825*
or PayPal to *sales@bookjungle.com*

Please contact us for bulk discounts

DIRECT-ORDER TERMS

**20% Discount if You Order
Two or More Books**
Free Domestic Shipping!
Accepted: Master Card, Visa,
Discover, American Express

www.ingramcontent.com/pod-product-compliance
Lightning Source LLC
Chambersburg PA
CBHW081328040426
42453CB00013B/2330